T0326816

THE UNIVERSITY AND THE NEW WORLD

This is the first volume in the Invitation Lecture Series of York University and it is an auspicious beginning. Three leaders in higher education in the United States here present their thoughts on challenging questions of enrolment, curriculum, and standards which today confront the ever expanding universities of North America. Professor Jones describes "The Idea of a University Once More"; Professor Riesman outlines and comments on some significant recent "Experiments in Higher Education"; Professor Ulich discusses a theme which is vitally important for the effect of university education, "Creativity."

HOWARD MUMFORD JONES is Abbott Lawrence Lowell Professor of the Humanities at Harvard University. He has been at Harvard since 1936, but has also taught at state universities in Texas, Montana, North Carolina and Michigan. He is the author of poetry, biography, drama and literary criticism; probably his best known work is *The Pursuit of Happiness*.

DAVID RIESMAN is the Henry Ford II Professor of the Social Sciences at Harvard University. He has studied biochemistry, law, psychiatry, government, economics and American history, has practised law in Boston, taught it at the University of Buffalo and spent a year in the New York County District Attorney's office. He is the author of a great number of books, essays and articles, including the provocative *The Lonely Crowd*.

ROBERT ULICH is the James Bryan Conant Professor of Education Emeritus at Harvard University. Born in Bavaria and educated in European universities, Professor Ulich joined the faculty of Harvard in 1934. He was Professor of Education and also taught in the Department of History of Science and Learning, and in the Divinity School. Among his works are *History of Educational Thought* and *The Education of Nations*.

YORK UNIVERSITY
Invitation Lecture Series
1962

THE *University*

AND THE *New World*

HOWARD MUMFORD JONES

DAVID RIESMAN

ROBERT ULICH

Published in association with
YORK UNIVERSITY
by UNIVERSITY OF TORONTO PRESS

© *University of Toronto Press* 1962
REPRINTED 2017
ISBN 978-1-4875-9212-7 (paper)

Foreword

A NEW university has a special opportunity and obligation to review the position of higher education in the modern world and to build into its structure, at the very beginning, certain innovations that seem relevant on the basis of this examination.

This is the primary reason for the topics and speakers selected in the first York University Lecture Series. We recognized, of course, that there was deep interest among the public in the questions we were examining and we were happy to invite many from the community to attend our lectures, but we wished ourselves, first of all, to see the problems of the University through the minds of men of deep insight and long academic experience.

The response of the public was, however, beyond our expectations and we are happy to share the lectures now with an even wider audience. The lectures, which were delivered in the late autumn of 1961 and the early winter of 1962, have been modified slightly as they have been prepared for publication.

One need hardly say that the analysis presented by our distinguished lecturers has stimulated great intellectual ferment at York and that their contribution to the thinking and the development of this University has been most significant.

MURRAY G. ROSS
President

Contents

The Idea of a University
Once More

Howard Mumford Jones

Howard Mumford Jones

Howard Mumford Jones is Abbott Lawrence Lowell Professor of the Humanities, Harvard University. He has been at Harvard since 1936 but has also taught at state universities in Texas, Montana, North Carolina and Michigan. He is the author of poetry, biography, drama and literary criticism. He is also the editor of many collections and anthologies. Probably his best known work is The Pursuit of Happiness, *although his own favourite is* The Harp That Once—*a life of Tom Moore.*

I AM honoured by the invitation to come to York University and participate, however remotely, in the shaping of a new institution. As an American I face a difficulty. Canada and the United States resemble each other in so many important particulars, it is difficult for Americans to remember that, except for Quebec, we are separated by a common language.

Now, a common language is a language that is commonly misunderstood. In the many areas of misunderstanding one of the most treacherous is higher education. When the American utters the word "university," he has no abiding image, or rather he has a kaleidoscopic image, of convenience rather than a philosophic one of weight. The word with us is applied to the oldest institution in the country, to a military school in Vermont, and to institutions of no standing at all. Our state legislatures are obliging, and consequently they will charter as a university anything that is not patently fraudulent. Small denominational colleges begin as universities or become so with no perceptible increase in equipment, and a passion to acquire the title breaks out among our state teachers colleges, which, having dropped "teacher" from their names, seek next to be transformed into universities.

The definition followed by the United States Office of Education is that a university is an institution of higher learning consisting of a liberal arts college offering graduate studies in a variety of fields and supporting at least two professional schools not exclusively technological. This is a paper definition only. The Office of Education, following its rules, could find only 141 universities in my country, but in 1959, 266 universities in the United States conferred the doctor's degree in course. To add to the confusion, institutions that do not call themselves universities—for example, Bryn Mawr College—do university work; and it is inconceivable that schools like the Massachusetts Institute of Technology should be stricken from the roll by an official definition.

You must, said Nietzsche, have chaos within you if you are to give birth to a dancing star. Whether the United States has any stellar choreographers in education is debatable, but remembering the injunction of Ortega y Gasset, "Let us look abroad for information, but not for a model," I think the most useful thing I can do is to discuss some of the pressing problems before American universities and draw some lessons from them.

Our institutions are usually classified as either public or private; that is, supported chiefly by tax money in the one case and by private endowment in the other. This is sometimes felt to be a primary distinction. Without denying its centrality and without entering the labyrinthine problem of university support, I venture to doubt that in 1961 the distinction is as important as it was in 1911. The weight and onset of our university problems lie elsewhere. Some state institutions—for instance Virginia and Michigan—exhibit many qualities associated with private universities, and some private universities—for example Cornell and the University of Pennsylvania—take on some functions connected with state universities. It is argued that, as taxation increases, private universities will have greater difficulty in maintaining themselves, but so many resources have been opened to them—government subsidies, grants from foundations, endowment drives, and so on—I doubt that American private colleges as a class are nearing extinction. It is more important that all our universities are subjected to common pressures and face common problems. I can summarize these in a single word: multitudinousness.

MULTITUDINOUSNESS: PRESSURE OF POPULATION

The most obvious creator of multitudinousness is the pressure of population. The figures, though familiar, are astonishing. In fifty years the population of my country has almost doubled—from a little more than 92 million in 1910 to more than 180 million in 1961. In 1910 the secondary school population of the United States was something more than a million, by 1951 six million, by 1961 about eleven million and a quarter. In 1910 our academic enrolment was about 50,000. In 1951 it was two million, and in 1961 it approached three and a quarter million. The number of high schools has increased, if not in parallel with the population, at least fast enough to keep up with need, but since it is more difficult to create a college overnight than a high school, it will not surprise you to learn that whereas in 1910 there were 581 institutions of higher learning in the United States, in 1960 this number was only 1,952. The secondary school population from which college students come grew in half a century in the proportion of twelve to one, but the number of academic institutions increased in the ratio of about three and a half to one. In 1910, 581 institutions of higher learning accommodated about 50,000 students; in 1960 less than 2,000 such institutions had to accommodate about three and a quarter million, an increase of the order of about 65 to one.

American universities have had perforce to alter their ways. When I was an undergraduate at the University of Wisconsin we thought, in 1912, that Madison was over-crowded with some 4,000 students. Today we read of universities with enrolments running to ten, twenty, twenty-five, thirty, and forty thousand. An institution like the University of California, while retaining its corporate identity, can scarcely create new campuses or hire instructors fast enough to keep up with demographic pressure. It plans on 170,000 students in all its branches by 1975.

Increase of student population has its effect upon the institution. A beginning course in psychology numbering 75 is one thing, a beginning course of 1,000 is something different. Instruction alters, radical changes are made in laboratory work, reading assignments, term papers, examinations, and much else. Following the principle that a fleet sails no faster than its slower vessels, it happens also that standards lower in proportion as the number of students rises. This lowering is inevitable in lecture courses, since it is virtually an acoustical law that the larger the group addressed, the less subtle the lecturer can hope to be. Nuances possible in water-colour must be replaced by effects possible only on a billboard.

I think we can grapple with large classes, if not with entire success, yet with some hope of alleviating the effects of mass. A deeper difficulty lies not in numbers but in change of expectation. Fifty years ago, to have graduated from high school was in itself proof of excellence. Today high school has lost its savour, and expectation among the ambitious is for a college degree. High schools were once terminal educational units with college preparatory attachments; nowadays this has changed. I do not mean that the American high school has lost its identity, I mean only that for an increasing fraction of its graduates high school is not enough. In some states, as a consequence—Ohio is an example—the state university is required by law to admit any graduate of any high school in the state, and it requires considerable ingenuity to retain university standards. A bachelor's degree takes on the significance formerly attached to a high school diploma.

This pressure requires many universities to devise means of dealing with an undifferentiated mass. If state universities are required to matriculate high school graduates, they must invent appropriate instruction. They develop special curriculums, such as that known as the general college. Simultaneously they must deal with graduates of junior colleges who, after two years in these schools, have a right to apply to the universities and complete their baccalaureate work. This situation increases the tendency to teach or reteach subjects that belong in secondary education, and obviously weakens the concept of a university as an institution of higher learning. Doubtless gigantism has been forced upon many American institutions, it has not been deliberately sought for, but I can utter no more sincere hope for York than that it will not have to face this kind of demographic democracy.

MULTITUDINOUSNESS: VOCATIONALISM

Another element making for multitudinousness is vocationalism. We are experiencing an increased demand, not always put in so many words, that universities shall train for jobs. Here, again, one must distinguish. At no time have all the students in all the universities attended for the pure love of learning; and even of medieval universities it can be said, I suspect, that going to Paris or Oxford was as frequently a search for preferment in church or state as it was an expression of *amor scientiae*. It is also true that in the eighteenth and nineteenth centuries, Western universities unwittingly developed into class institutions. Poor boys attended them, but universities were coloured by the predilection of the establishment to remain established, so that the sizar did not receive the attention given the son of a nobleman. Snobbery lingered into our own time, unless I misread *The Landlord at Lion's Head* by William Dean Howells and *Jude the Obscure* by Thomas Hardy. In the nineteenth century, nevertheless, the proponents of liberal education as a goal were vigorous and influential—witness Newman, Arnold, Charles W. Eliot and Woodrow Wilson —and the formal aim of any university always remained liberal. A liberal education has been variously defined— William James said it was that sort of education which enabled you to tell a good man when you saw him—but it was generally held that a university degree certified you were on the road to filling any of the offices, public or private, whether of peace or of war.

A theoretical liberal aim has not vanished from American universities. The faculty of arts and sciences is still central, and homage is paid to liberal education by deans in schools of commerce and law and medicine and public health and veterinary science. But the ideal has been attenuated in the confusion between professional education and vocational training. The argument is simplicity itself. If a university properly offers degrees in divinity, law, and medicine, why should it not also offer degrees in such newer professions as commerce, public health, pharmacology, animal husbandry, and so forth? And if it offers degrees in these laudable skills, why, by the same token, should it refuse to give instruction in writing TV shows, playground management, cooking, stenography, dress-making, and automobile driving? It is useless to argue that training in such skills should be offered somewhere else. You are at once confronted with a democratic, not to say populist, theory of culture. You don't want to discriminate among honest employments, do you? That would be unfair. You don't want to confine the blessings of higher learning to an élite, do you? That would be aristocratical. I do not know whether you have these arguments in Canada, but the consequence in my country is that at a Commencement ceremony in some one of our large universities, you will see conferred a variety of degrees that exhaust the alphabet. The centrality of the university ideal tends to merge into a general educational kaleidoscope, and the physical resources of the plant dissipate into work-rooms, laboratory theatres, visual art experiment stations, special libraries of tapes, radio stations and cooking classes. I am therefore happy to see York University in its calendar dedicate itself to the liberal aims.

MULTITUDINOUSNESS: EXPERTISE

A third force for multitudinousness is the American demand for *expertise*. It is difficult to distinguish among the professional man, the specialist, and the expert, and I shall not embark upon this dark, metaphysical task. The definition of an American university is, as I have said, that it shall include a liberal college offering graduate education and at least two professional schools not exclusively technological. The union of a faculty of the liberal arts and two such professional schools assumes that professional training should have some relation to a philosophic point of view. Contrast all this with an American TV and radio show called "Stump the Experts." The TV and radio show made no such assumption. *Expertise* appeared principally as a peculiar form of memory, and the experts were stumped competitively—a method which is philosophic only in a Pickwickian sense. They were stumped not because they were unable to show the relevance to Machiavelli to the Cold War or to clarify the relation between atomic physics and absolute truth—this they were never asked to do; they were stumped when they could not remember the names of nine American states having a town named Odessa or got the wrong author for the immortal: "From Saskatoon, Saskatchewan, to Walla Walla, Wash."

Now, educating certain sorts of technicians—dental hygienists, social workers, physical therapists, public school teachers is not necessarily a function of graduate education. But inasmuch as these honourable vocations yearn to become professions, a tendency develops to require something better for entrance into them than a B.A. degree—a master's degree in the first instance and by and by the doctorate. Formal tribute is always paid to the doctrine that education should be philosophic, but the doctor's degree thus administered tends to become a degree in *expertise* rather than a professional degree in learning. Nor is the tendency to *expertise* confined to newer vocations. It affects degree programmes long established. With us, for example, about 20 per cent of the annual crop of Ph.D.'s in chemistry go into university work, most of the others taking posts in industry or government, where the mastery of new knowledge sometimes takes shape as "group-think" or the random collision of mind with mind.

As we need chemists, mathematicians, geologists, engineers, physicists, economic analysts, personnel directors and so on, where are they to originate if not in our graduate or professional schools? But the argument is baffling. On the one hand, it is charged that getting a professional degree takes too long; on the other hand, it is solemnly pointed out that the advance of knowledge in all fields is swifter than ever. We have the comment that our young expert does not know enough and in the same breath the comment that the faculty takes too much time to teach him what little he knows. It is a fixed belief among many industrialists that the pace of technical development means that only on-the-job training can acquaint the beginner with present developments; but it is also their fixed belief that too much time is spent in professional curriculum on theory and not enough time on practice. How to reconcile the two parts of an antilogy, at least as old as Aristotle, to a clientele in *expertise* that knows not Aristotle I cannot say.

MULTITUDINOUSNESS: RESEARCH FOR DEFENCE
AND INDUSTRY

I turn to a last component of our multitudinousness. Industry and government find that universities are excellent places in which to get research done—research necessary for either the development or the defence of the country. Much of this research leads to basic general knowledge; much of it does not. All these projects are effected through special contracts running for a shorter or longer period and requiring either the creation of a special staff or the delegation of faculty members to that purpose. These projects sometimes have budgets permitting their directors to offer attractive fellowships to graduate students and to secure the services of young Ph.D.'s. The size of the personnel and the terms of service vary widely. The staff of the Smithsonian Institution division for astrophysics at my own university runs to over 300 and includes members of our faculty, but other projects may need only five or six persons. In 1959–1960 government support of projects at Harvard ran to over 18 million dollars, most of it going into science, some of it going into the social sciences, and none of it (excepting $80,000 for Eastern languages) going into the humanities. Both industrial and government contracts often include a secrecy clause, or a first-user clause, requiring whatever is discovered to be kept from general knowledge for a stipulated period of time.

Such agreements deny one of the major promises of our dedication to the advance of knowledge since they shut up discovery for the use of a few and deny it to the general community. For this reason some institutions will sign no contract with a secrecy clause. Even then, the creation of these conclaves within, yet apart from, the total university creates special problems. When the project is ended, what is the responsibility of the institution for the professional future of their staffs? If I add to these transient units other extra-curricular foundations that are permanent in intention —titles like the Institute for African Studies, the Russian Research Centre, the Forest Products Laboratory are characteristic—it is evident that the traditional picture of a university as a body of students and masters pursuing the higher branches of learning and having the corporate power to confer degrees upon properly qualified persons, has suffered a change. None of these projects can be defended. Yet the movement they create is centrifugal, not centripetal, the core of the university idea tends to be smothered by non-university responsibilities, and in the States, at least, a university tends more and more to be defined by the variety of things it does, and not by what it is. Here again is a force making for confusion.

Such, then, are some of the components of multitudinousness in American universities. These forces make for a weakening of the university ideal and of the ideal of a democratic culture. This is not the common opinion. The common opinion runs in precisely the contrary direction. The argument is that the state is endangered by the Communist world in the cold war and therefore the university is obliged to contribute its imagination and its training in *expertise* to create new instruments of defence or of attack. Where else shall these instruments be invented? How else shall they be brought into being if not by university-trained experts—the very men who created the atom bomb? It is likewise argued that an industrial culture must maintain and, if possible, advance its means of production to some indefinite, but receding, limit.

It must do this both to make its own people happy and to distribute happiness to under-developed countries. Much, therefore, is made of the contributions that departments of economics and anthropology, colleges of commerce and schools of education, chemical laboratories, engineering schools, and so on, can make towards inventing new goods, new machines to make new goods, new ways to make new machines run faster with fewer men to attend them, new money to pay for the new workers, the new machines, the new distribution and the new goods. That happiness might in certain instances lie in remaining undeveloped areas is not a credible idea, despite the constant flight of tourists to the South Seas, the Greek Islands, and other parts of the world more pastoral than Mannheim, Birmingham, or Gary, Indiana.

These arguments have cogency, and flatly to deny them is to argue that one is either impractical or unpatriotic. I have no desire to acquire the halo of martyrdom. Still, one may reasonably inquire whether the invention and manufacture of lethal weapons is a true function of a university as this term has hitherto been understood. I seem to remember that the University of Berlin was founded in the midst of the Napoleonic wars without reference to martial matters and with a dedication to *Lehrfreiheit* and *Lernfreiheit*, ideals that were much admired in their time. One may also reasonably inquire whether the increase and distribution of economic goods is a main goal of university work. I seem unable to make this aim jibe with the picture of Oxford, that home of lost causes, all her dreaming spires now vibrating with the motor traffic. Perhaps, however, the traditional notion of a university is a lost cause. What can a university really do for us in these parlous times?

DIFFICULTIES OF EXPERTISE AS UNIVERSITY WORK

Among the components of multitudinousness I found *expertise* most important; that is, the training of experts by the university. Obviously *expertise* is essential both to defence and to industry. They would shrivel without it. Hitherto, of course, we have tended to confine military *expertise* to our service schools, and it is just possible we would be wiser to develop service schools to the point of furnishing this kind of *expertise* than to warp our universities. A minority of thoughtful people are beginning at least to ask the question, and a recent suggestion is that we should create special institutions devoted only to this purpose.

But let us consider *expertise* in its more peaceful connotation. Why is not *expertise* a proper object of university training? Well, in some sense it is a proper object of university training, but it should not be the whole object of university training, only a subordinate part, a side effect. *Expertise* seems to me to fail of being true university work for three reasons: it has, on the whole, rather more of a commercial flavour than a cultural one; it is on the whole a means, not an end; and it can get along, unfortunately, without any moral commitment outside itself.

Expertise, however necessary to industry and commerce, is overwhelmingly practical and but dimly philosophic. It is, in truth, only the vocational raised to a higher level. Vocational education can be valuable education, and I think even university education ought to have some relation to livelihood. Nevertheless, I suggest that to confuse vocational training with university education is, in Sir Thomas Browne's phrase, a vulgar error, and, moreover, a vulgar error constantly being made. It is made, for example, whenever educators solemnly assure simple-minded taxpayers that a college man *ipso facto* earns more money than does a non-college man. It is also made whenever high school teachers come up to the university, as they quaintly say, to "take more work," meaning that they hope to go back eligible for an increase in salary. The result is our dreamy summer-school graduate courses constructed for high school teachers. These courses embody two fallacies. One is the fallacy of compulsory chapel attendance, or the assumption that the best way to assure morality is to drive people to church; and the second is the fallacy that the principal difference between a graduate school in a university and a secretarial school is that the placement office of the secretarial school is more efficient in selling its wares.

The second great difficulty with *expertise* as the principal object of university work is that *expertise* is not an end in itself, though it is often considered to be so. Obviously it is better to have good engineers, good farmers, good chemists, and good economic analysts than bad engineers, and so on. By the same token it is better to have good horse jockeys, good bar tenders and good garage mechanics than it is to have bad ones. But the central issue is not a hierarchy of employment status, nor even goodness or badness of skill, the central problem is the problem of the goodness or badness of the end for which the skill is employed—a distinction as old as Plato but a distinction so blurred by our industrial culture that the president of the Carnegie Foundation had to publish a year or two ago a book devoted to the revolutionary idea that the aim of education in a democracy is not efficiency, but excellence.

The third difficulty of *expertise* is that it has no great system of moral reference outside itself. Within the confines of its system, ethical standards may be high. A well-trained engineer will not use inadequate materials, a well-trained architect will not put up shoddy buildings, a well-trained economic analyst will not alter his statistics to please the government, a well-trained journalist will not suppress a story to please a banker. But if you ask the journalist whether the newspaper informs or merely titillates the public; if you ask the analyst whether the aim of any economic system is wisdom and happiness or merely production and exchange, if you ask the architect why he adds to traffic congestion and the engineer whether his power system is not going to ruin the scenery, he is likely to say that this kind of thing is not his responsibility. Like the Apostle Paul the expert is forced to believe the higher powers are ordained of God and should be obeyed.

The men who managed Buchenwald and Dachau displayed, I dare say, *expertise* of a high order in their dreadful trade and were probably kind to their wives and children. I do not in the least mean to hint that our economists and engineers are likely to imitate these Satanic engines, but the extreme case has at least the sorry advantage of showing whither a road may lead; and a fundamental difficulty of *expertise* as an end in itself is that you can practice it with great efficiency and honesty inside or outside any moral code.

Let us not be scared by a digital computer, which is only a ventriloquist in disguise. When Milton called Athens the eye of Greece, I suspect he did not have in mind the superior *expertise* whereby Themistocles trapped the Persian fleet at Salamis; I think for Milton the glory that was Greece had more to do with Plato and Socrates, Aristotle and Euclid, Sophocles and Phidias, the Acropolis and the Academy. What somebody has called "the great discourse of Western man" began under the blue sky of Hellas, and this discourse it is the primary duty of universities to carry on. When a distinguished scientist assures me in print that, at a rough estimate, the progress of science would not be affected greatly if 80 per cent or 90 per cent of the articles now published were simply buried in the archives and not indexed; when I go through the files of my own learned journals and find the vast majority of specialized contributions are repetitive trivia, then I am prepared to be indulgent to the charge that specialization is a dead end, that what Dr. Alvin Weinberg calls Big Science does indeed create its own technical bosses, and that if, as Lord Home lately told us, man has at long last been possibly terrified into peace, now is a good time to inquire whether there is not a critical size for universities as well as for atomic bombs.

GREEK ROAD OR ROMAN ONE?

I suppose all universities must follow either the Greek road or the Roman one. If they elect the Roman road, as many of our big ones are forced to do, they become imperial powers with a president as remote as Augustus Caesar, an enormous administrative staff in turn administered by secretaries, a gigantic budget, faculties so big they cannot meet to transact business, students organized into squads,

platoons, companies, regiments, and brigades, catalogues
like encyclopaedias, and a physical plant that resembles
an army installation more than it does an ivory tower. Experts swarm, and *expertise* is the life of their moral being.
I am far from despising these colossi, but I find in them a
thirst for order that, like the organized Roman Empire, if
it conquered vast territories, by and by collapsed of extensi-
bility. Like our great foundations, they have vivid virtues
and vivid faults, among which unwieldiness, an inability
to experiment except formally in laboratories or expeditions
or special institutes, and a curious infertility in basic ideas
must be counted.

By "basic ideas" I do not mean the kind of research
work now rewarded by the Nobel prize; I mean that hazard
of volition William James found to be the first step towards
a new truth. I also borrow from James his fine, descriptive
phrase concerning "men who are strongly of the fact-loving
temperament" kept at a distance from idealism. I suggest
that universities of the Roman or imperial order are mainly
staffed by men who are strongly of the fact-loving temperament, and that is why they go in so strongly for *expertise.*

Schools of the Greek order—and here I shall not be pre-
cise in the meaning of "university"—are more flexible, less
hierarchical, not bound to regimentation, less interested in
dimension than in direction, less concerned with specialized
techniques than with what Principal James of McGill de-
nominates "the techniques of general ideas." In them, learning is a noun, not a participle attached to something else for
its meaning. They value discourse a little more and discovery a little less perhaps than do their Roman compeers,
but this does not mean that they lack interest in discovery
but only that they come to it from another angle of vision.
For them, the heart of the university is that which interprets
and transmits the system of values and predilections,
notions, and perhaps errors we describe as the culture of

the race—I paraphrase Meredith Wilson—and this culture they simultaneously support, transmit, and criticize. They do not believe that the future, even of an industrial society, lies wholly in the power of the technologists, or even of army engineers; on the contrary they are aware that technicians only serve the state, they do not direct it. Citizens direct it. Citizens need a governing philosophy, and this governing philosophy these schools conceive it their duty to conserve, to interpret, and to transmit.

I am almost ashamed to say that the source and the experimentation that give us this governing philosophy lie in the records and the experimentation of the race itself: in religion, in the arts, in law, in science, in philosophy, in the commerce of man with man and of nation with nation and of man and nation with nature. But I am not ashamed to utter this platitude because, misled by too much *expertise*, we academics too often ignore a patent truth. If this seems harsh, consider the impatience of the research scientist with anybody interested in history, even in the history of science, the repudiation of that part of the literary past they dislike—and they dislike most of it—by most of our academic literary critics, the blankness of vision with which philosophers, especially of the high and dry persuasion, glance at religion, or the inability of our social scientists in many fields really to conceive of any other norm for modern man than an industrialized order.

THINKING IS A MORAL ART

Universities of the Greek tradition as opposed to universities of the Roman imperial order are smaller; and smallness gives them the advantage of being able to hear the discourse of Western man above the noise of the machine shops. I congratulate you at York that this is so. You have historical precedent and contemporary analogue for avoiding gigantism. The contemporary analogue is the refusal of Dr. Michael Grant, vice-president of Queen's in Belfast, to commit himself or his institution to expansionism; the analogue is the creation of The Johns Hopkins University at Baltimore in 1876, a date from which we count our academic maturity in the United States. When it was begun, that institution had virtually no buildings, no laboratories, and no library, but it had a group of scholars determined to participate in the discourse I have denominated as proper to university life. Being fallible men, even as we, they were a little bemused by evolutionary theory, which they made the key to everything, but they insisted upon human dignity, they insisted upon intellectual freedom, they insisted upon the concept of the state as an intelligent and intelligible order, they insisted that historic change had meaning, and they refused to believe the principal value of evolutionary man was his survival value.

Some wise man has said that the art of thinking is not an intellectual art but a moral art. The moral arts do not flourish well in a context of confusion; and I can find nothing in my notion of a proper university that compels it to take on the confusion of multitudinousness. Is it not true that some of the dynamic intellectual centres of history have been rather small affairs? In the days when Plato was teaching in his Academy the total population of freemen in Athens was about 50,000—the enrolment in an institution like New York University today—of whom only a few score, in all probability, were, in our sense, students; yet of the so-called Old Academy and the academicans Cicero wrote: "Their writings and method contain all liberal learning, all history, all polite discourse, and . . . embrace such a variety of arts that no one can undertake any noble career without their aid." This may be a little excessive— Cicero tends to be excessive—but I prefer it as a university idea to the aim of *expertise*. The University of Göttingen was not large; yet in its heyday its influence was felt throughout the Western World. I have already spoken of The Johns Hopkins University.

Everyone repeats admiringly a tag from Goethe's *Torquato Tasso*:

> Es bildet ein Talent sich in der Stille,
> Sich ein Charakter in dem Strom der Welt—

Man's talent ripens in tranquillity, his character in battling with the world. Without entering into the problem of the relation between talent and character, I insist that at the heart of the university idea, if we are to develop talent, there should always be a centre of stillness. The instinct that located young colleges and universities of the New World in rural retreats was a sound instinct; and when the industrial city catches up and swallows these institutions, they change character, they lose something of value, some intangible, that quality that Arnold caught in his magical phrases about Oxford. Doubtless gigantic educational institutions are useful to an industrial culture, but do we all have to be gigantic? Is the only test of excellence in a university that it shall always be bigger? I plead for the small school and the stillness.

THE ACADEMY OF FINE IDEAS

Of course the cost of silence steadily rises in an epoch of transistor radios when even undertaking parlours are equipped with piped-in music. Observe, however, the irony of creating institutes of advanced study in quiet places where the scholar can go to escape the noise and bustle of university life. We sacrifice too much to service and we do not toil enough at salvation. If a university has any unique purpose that no other institution can quite fulfil, it is, or should be, as a place for weighing fundamental thoughts. They also serve who only stand and think. Indeed, it may be less important for a university to have a cyclotron than it is to have a soul. The protection of man thinking is the fundamental, the quintessential duty of universities; to this duty everything else is secondary and subordinate, even a gift for the endowment of a college of practical arts. We need to remember that significance of the title of one of Wallace Stevens' poems: *The Academy of Fine Ideas.*

I heartily hope that York University may long continue in its dedication to the humanizing of man, freeing him, in the words of your President's inaugural address, from those pressures which mechanize the mind and which permit custom to dominate intelligence. This is admirably said, it is said in the great tradition of intellectual idealism that stretches from Plato through Aquinas to Emerson and Newman. The humanizing of man is the central need in a time when technicians are happily engaged dehumanizing him with dispatch and efficiency. If over the years York University will but cling staunchly to an idealism no longer fashionable in the world of the existentialists, it will be of great and increasing value to Canada, to the New World, and to that nobler doctrine: of man and of the state we tend to forget in the clatter of our typewriters, our voting machines, our loud speakers, our airplanes and, sad thunder over all, the terrible wild energy of our atom bombs.

Experiments in Higher
Education

David Riesman

David Riesman

*David Riesman is the Henry Ford II Professor of the Social
Sciences, Harvard University. He has had a varied career
indeed. He studied bio-chemistry, law, psychiatry, government, economics and American history—among other subjects. He practised law in Boston, taught it at the University
of Buffalo and spent a year in the New York County District Attorney's office. For three years he was an official of
the Sperry Gyroscope Company. He has been interested
in dairy farming since 1931, and he and his family still
live on a Vermont dairy farm in summer. He is the author
of a great number of books, essays and articles, probably
the best known of which is* The Lonely Crowd: A Study of
the Changing American Character.

I WANT to talk today about something that I hope is relevant for York and its setting; namely, the recent decades of experiments and senescence in higher education. In the period of the 1930's which coincided with a period of social ferment, the great debates which were conducted in the national forum, for instance, between New Dealers and anti-New Dealers, or between Fascists and anti-Fascists, were conducted within the educational forum, let us say, between the pro- and anti-Robert Hutchins forces or the pro- and anti-Alexander Meiklejohn forces.

THE VANISHING CAPTAIN OF ERUDITION

This was an era, perhaps the last era in American universities, of the Great Man President. The Great Man President has been a feature of American higher education for 100 years, going back to men like Henry Tappan at the University of Michigan in the 1850's, or Charles Eliot at Harvard, and a little later, the founders of Johns Hopkins and other institutions of the late nineteenth century. In the thirties there were on the scene descendants, metaphorical descendants, of those nineteenth-century greats: men like Clarence Cook Little, again at Michigan, or Abbott Lawrence Lowell at Harvard, and Hutchins himself. Captains of Erudition, Veblen would have called them. There were also, at this time, men who founded new colleges—mostly small: Sarah Lawrence, Black Mountain, Bennington—or who took over previously moribund colleges like Antioch or Swarthmore or Bard and made in effect new institutions out of them.[1]

I think it might be contended that there is no room any more for the Great Man university president except in "backward" institutions. Increasingly, the president of the

[1] I am indebted to the Carnegie Corporation for support in studying higher education.

modern ramified university becomes, whether he wishes it or not, a finagler between the budget lines, who can exercise only the most modest and incremental influence. A few manage to face both outward to the community and its various publics and inward across the faculty and its various divisions along departmental, gerontocratic, political and other lines. Occasionally, the outward-turning president may leave room for an inward-turning dean to influence the direction and speed of change, especially where over-all growth allows some freedom of manoeuvre. On the whole, however, the Great Man President has been succeeded by the Distinguished Department Chairman, who makes the Great Man President obsolete. This, indeed, is accompanied by the rise of the great universities as the dominant features of the academic landscape, and of research, and of what might be called, in the terms of Michael Young, the meritocracy or the diploma élite.

THE HEGEMONY OF RESEARCH

The average Princeton professor of engineering and science today controls an annual budget of $120,000, and such a man is not going to be subordinate to a president. Presidents come and go, and such a man, if he has a Nobel prize particularly, is an attractive commodity for inter-academic rivalry. A few such men have been lured by the opportunity to become a research professor; this again is a new phenomenon: the research professor who rises above the "mere" teaching of students other than apprentices. The model created by the great research-oriented universities is spreading nearly everywhere in the States. Wesleyan University, for instance, has always been a good small college—not so very small—a very rich and well-endowed and enterprising one, and has become a recent convert to the idea that if you are going to be a distinguished college you have to have a graduate school. Many of the small colleges in the United States feel their days are numbered, unless they can move towards the university model and keep good faculty members by providing them with graduate students (who will also teach and monitor the undergraduates).[2]

Now, at the same time that this development has occurred, the increasing tendency among the best and brightest undergraduates in American institutions of higher learning is to go on to graduate school, and I mean the graduate school of arts and sciences. Thus the man who is teaching in the undergraduate college is more and more training people as recruits to his own field or hoped-for recruits to his own field, and this process takes priority over undergraduate experimentation because he is sending men on who will be judged by their ability to meet the payrolls in the departments to which they go as graduate students, and by their ability to get into those departments. In other words, whereas, at the lower levels in the high schools and preparatory schools today, the pressure of getting into college affects, if not the curriculum in its details, at least the style of work, so that most headmasters and secondary school principals feel that they will be judged by their customers—that is, the children and their parents—by their ability to get into the best colleges, so the colleges are beginning to become—and I speak only of the top institutions—prep schools for the graduate schools.

At Harvard in the last several years 86 to 90 per cent of the students have gone on to graduate work of one sort or another, and this completely changes the character of

[2]In connection with the foregoing, President James S. Coles of Bowdoin College has pointed out to me the possibility of a small college offering graduate study in several selected fields (as Bryn Mawr College does), perhaps especially in those where the great universities' post-doctoral fellows tend increasingly to crowd out the graduate students themselves. If the fields were carefully chosen, the undergraduate college might be strengthened rather than becoming subordinated to the full panoply of graduate activities.

the undergraduate degree. I doubt if this has happened in Canada so fully yet, and I hope in discussions and questions which will follow my formal talk, we may perhaps explore differences between your situation and that south of the border. But at any rate, once the college becomes judged as a prep school for a graduate school, its character as a place of exploration and experiment naturally changes. The experiments themselves appear enormously time-consuming in a situation in which the departments are strengthened by the fact that they are engaged in research and that they are training people who will go on in graduate work. Then the task of integrating the specialties of American academic life becomes about as difficult as integrating the Armed Services or the United Nations.

Indeed, any integration that occurs among seemingly neighbouring fields tends to cut them off from fields that in some perspectives may be thought no less relevant. I am, for instance, a member of the Department of Social Relations at Harvard. This is an experiment which began in 1946 as a part of the post-war excitement in the social sciences, bringing together sociology, social-anthropology, and social and clinical (or personality) psychology. But the effort to bring together these sub-departments, which should never have been separated in the first place, encounters the danger of consuming so much energy as to cut us off from philosophy, from economics or government, and from biology.

So it is understandable for a young man, who is coming on in one of the academic fields, to reject the effort at integration, and the effort at undergraduate experiment that may be linked with integration, because he feels that the exciting call of his sub-specialty leads him more quickly to interesting and non-controversial work.

Moreover, there is a strange paradox in the fate of the academic man in the United States; namely, that if he becomes too dedicated to his institution he may be victimized by it because he has no mobility within his field. If he is known as a "good Joe," adored by the students, a hard worker who carries out his committee work and is helpful in working in the local not the guild-national academic enterprise, he becomes like a parish priest who will never become a bishop. He is lost to the call from elsewhere that will strengthen his position in his own institution. So a man in academic life who devotes himself to the institution soon may be gobbled up by that very institution, for then he is like the wife who has become dowdy: he has not retained social mobility. Furthermore, the changes in the problems posed for education by the changes in our society—so that the college generations change faster than other generations, even faster sometimes than once in four years—mean that the person who is interested in students, and concerned with their development, faces a task of understanding the material he is working with, the human material, which is extremely demanding and taxing; whereas the person who is facing only the problems of his specialty and its development can proceed in a more unequivocal way and with less ambiguity.

So much for the background into which I want to set a few experiments that I propose to use for illustrative purposes tonight. I am going to divide these experiments into two groups: one, experiments in the Ivy League—on the whole, well-heeled, traditional, private universities of the Eastern Seaboard; and the other, experiments in public education in the state university systems. In each of these, I think the problems are different, and what is needed is different, and I want to illustrate this by a few examples.

THE FRESHMAN SEMINARS AT HARVARD

I want to speak first about an experiment in which I have had an active hand, the Freshman Seminar Program at Harvard which began three years ago, and which opened to freshmen a small, ungraded seminar, which would be one-half or one-fourth of their program in the first year, and would depart from the large General Education courses which are the general freshman fare at Harvard. This is similar to a plan which is outlined for York but not yet in effect—of having, in the upper-class years, an ungraded but credit-giving course or seminar in which the student can explore some new aspect of himself and the world.

The Freshman Seminar Program, like other experiments, appears to have been the result of a conjunction of three potent forces: a group of faculty men and administrators who had been drafting plans for improving the freshman year; money from a generous and far-seeing donor; and a talented administrator.

The group that had been concerned with the freshman year was a very small one, as we would expect in the light of the competing preoccupations of university faculties on which I've already touched. However, its ideas as to what might be done turned out to be congruent with the ideas of a donor who was himself vitally interested in education. And the administrator, Dean McGeorge Bundy, sensitive to the temper of the present anti-ideological mood, helped steer the program through the faculty by minimizing debate over large educational issues and by emphasizing the fact that the program was to have a short trial run only and be subject to careful faculty review.[3] Thus the faculty were not put into the position of having to argue out what was the "problem" of the freshman year or indeed if there was a problem.

In principle, moreover, the program was permissive: any senior faculty member was entitled to offer a Freshman Seminar. In practice, however, invitations were issued to

[3]For fuller discussion of a somewhat analogous case compare my article, "Planning in Higher Education: Some Notes on Patterns and Problems," *Human Organization*, volume 18, no. 1, pp. 12–17.

faculty members encouraging them to offer seminars—and now in the program's third year the problem is often one of finding enough capable men who will undertake a seminar in the face of competing obligations. Thus, as a result of self-selection and recruitment of faculty, not all the divergent, if tacit, philosophies of education represented at Harvard were represented in the Freshman Seminars as actually offered, but understandably the seminars that were offered represented different approaches depending on the different men who led them. Some professors established that, by pre-selecting students who had won national American scholarships (or Westinghouse Science Talent Fair Exhibitors), one could in effect move freshmen into graduate school immediately. Others tried to deal with small groups who were doing writing, or interested in drama, and they had a rather different experience.

I believe that, whatever the seminar experience, it was a good experience on the whole because it was new. I was suggesting this afternoon to some of the York students some advantages of newness, that the "Hawthorne Plant effect" operated in any new enterprise; that is, the fact that people were starting fresh, that you were a charter member, that you had a sense of taking part in something that was not the three-hundredth run of it, gave a certain vitality to novel operations. And this was true of the Freshman Seminar students. The reasons given for the diversity of faculty approach to the seminars reflect the different definitions by academicians of what is the "problem" of the freshman year at an institution like Harvard. Some defined it as the problem of the blasé student who comes to Harvard already highly prepared, from a school like Exeter, St. Mark's, or one of the better New York City or suburban high schools; and has known many people, often including family members, who have attended Harvard. He comes to Harvard thinking he knows what it is like, discovers often too late that he is mistaken and that he may have to become a different sort of person if he is to live up to its expectations and his own. This complex combination of over-preparation, under-anticipation, early condescension and beginning self-mistrust, apparent indifference and underlying anxiety, has sometimes at Harvard been called "the Exeter Syndrome" (though not all would define it as I have just done); however defined, it is one of the named sources of difficulty that had been under discussion at the time the seminar program was adumbrated.

Another source of difficulty is quite different. It is represented for me by a student in the Freshman Seminar that Dorothy Lee and I led three years ago. When by chance I sat down next to him at one of our first dinner meetings, it turned out that he came from a far Western town where his father ran a motel, and he had been, as probably half our students have been, valedictorian at high school. This was a small high school, of whose graduating class he was the only one not to stay within the state for higher education, and the second one to have come to Harvard. He was in a chemistry course, he told me. Chemistry had been his best course at high school, and now he was doing more poorly in chemistry than boys from better high schools who had never had any chemistry before. So I said, "It looks as though perhaps you are in the wrong university." He said, "I am, but the band played when I left and I can't go back."

The Freshman Seminar Program, in the minds of some of us, was in part an effort to reach and react to such students who represent the institution's efforts towards democratization and geographic distribution, and to understand and perhaps moderate the ensuing casualties. One of the things which this type of Freshman Seminar Program did was to remove the sense of great impersonality that some of the students have in an institution like Harvard, with 5,500 men and women undergraduates. By state university standards, this is not huge, but it is larger than most American Ivy League colleges. The seminars gave these students a sense of access to faculty. Partly, I think, this access has a mythical quality, a feeling that a small group is necessarily personal and close; but it is a mythical quality in which people devoutly believe, and which gives a sense of belonging provided in other institutions by fraternities and various other groupings having their own woebegone deficiencies.

Still another problem, it seemed to me, was more important. For my experience of the Freshman Seminar was that it took the students out of that one area of C. P. Snow's "two cultures" in which he had previously defined himself, and it gave him a chance to look at the other area or areas. The reason I think this is increasingly important is that, as we become more of a meritocracy—as we tighten up in a kind of post-sputnik educational acceleration game—we see that, at our best institutions, the intellect has won out, the academic has won out, and therefore the problems that loom ahead of us are not the problems that were faced by an older generation of professors who worried that the students were "collegiate" and indolent and paid no attention to them.

The problem often seems to take the following form: a young man who comes to a high-prestige, selective institution has, from the ninth grade onward or even before, defined himself as heading for college—and for a good college—and in the course of that, has said, "I am a this, I am a that, I am (let us say) a chemistry-concentrator." This decision on his part has simplified his life when people ask him what he wants to do; and it has drawn to him his chemistry teacher in high school, who may also coach sports and is probably the only rigorous teacher to whom he can respond who is also male (whereas of course, as you know, in the American high school—and the American elementary school even more—the boy is faced largely by women, and may define the arts as "women's subjects").[4]

At any rate, he is a chemist; he likes to mess around in the basement, his parents think he is headed for chemistry or medicine, and these are "okay" things. When he comes into college, he still sees himself as a chemist, and he sees his task as re-establishing his adequacy which he has demonstrated in high school. If anything but chemistry gets in his way, it prevents him from establishing that he is adequate. On the other side of C. P. Snow's "divide," one gets, let us say, a very bright girl for whom the sciences would be defeminizing: who has defined herself as interested in fine arts or English, who regards science as fit only for barbarians and engineers, and it is not for her. She has staked her adequacy as a woman and as an intellect on her literary or artistic gifts. She, too, comes to college, not to shake up that definition, but to re-affirm it under pressure.

In this endless roller-coaster of American and Canadian education, in which you go up to the sixth grade and then go down again in Junior High, then up again and then down again, then you start all over again in graduate school—in this roller-coaster system, the freshman is at the bottom again and has to define himself, or herself, as competent and adequate in a new *milieu*. Such considerations led me to describe one task of the seminar of which I was the leader, as that of taking a person, in whichever of these two cultures he or she had defined himself or herself, and saying: "You are required to look across the divide, and to question its depth and reality. You are not allowed here to regard one as the Humanities and the other as the Sciences.

[4]This is probably an overstatement as far as the American high school is concerned where the sciences, shop subjects, and sometimes history and even English are taught by men. There are considerable differences here from year to year and region to region; and of course the private preparatory schools, like their British models, have a male faculty. But it remains traditionally true in America, reminiscent of the days of Tom Sawyer, that culture, the arts, civility tend to be associated by boys with their mothers and school marms.

We are going to break down these dichotomies. We are going to look at them. We will present to you the kind of people and ideas and problems that the different fields of knowledge present, so that you can re-decide for yourself whether your early and premature closure is a good one or one that you want to re-examine." It turned out that many did re-examine their early definitions of themselves. They also re-examined their definition of those with whom they could enjoy talking, and many of the friendships that grew up in the seminar's informal life crossed the divides that usually separate undergraduates from each other.

THE PROJECTED SENIOR CENTRE AT BOWDOIN

This consideration of the need to define adequacy has made me especially interested in one program which has not yet seen the light of day, and is in the planning stage; that is, the projected senior year at Bowdoin College, a small college in one of our "Maritime Provinces." The plan, as I understand it, is based on the idea that the first three years are given over to the effort of the student to establish his adequacy in his department, in a fraternity, and in other sometimes ritualistic activities. In the fourth year, before he is given his degree, the student will not only continue his specialized work in his department but will take part in a Senior Colloquium that is as yet not fully worked out but is intended to cut across the fields of knowledge. Whether, after a person has decided who he is for three years, he will be ready then to broaden out again and to lift his focus from his new-found competence in a specialty, building on that competence in more complicated ways than mere extrapolation, remains of course to be explored. However, as already indicated, I think there is much to be gained from exploring the possibilities of putting General Education in the fourth year, rather than in the first year. Not only can it build then on an already confirmed sense of acquired confidence and on an apprenticeship in certain areas, but it can implicitly say to the student that General Education in the broadest sense is something that is an obligation for the whole of life, not something to be got out of the way in the freshman year. Indeed I think in general that we pay too little attention to what college implicity says to those who attend it about what is going to be their attitude towards non-required learning throughout the rest of their lives.

These two experiments, one in the freshman year and one in the final year—each of them ambiguous in its message and one of them still to be tried out—must serve here for illustrative purposes of what is going on in some of the older institutions of the Atlantic Seaboard. I mentioned one other, the colleges at Wesleyan, with which I have spent some time, which take a youngster in his sophomore year for three years of highly intensive work, in a college whose aim is to cut across certain neighbouring fields. So there is a college of behavioural sciences, which, as I recall, includes psychology, anthropology, philosophy and history, for instance; and a college of humanities, which includes some of the same and some different fields, in which the students work with enormous intensity; these are small residential colleges but not like the Oxford or Cambridge colleges, which muster the various fields. The Wesleyan colleges draw people who intend to concentrate, not in a narrow department but in a series of neighbouring fields, with faculty members also in those fields. This experiment has only recently begun. And there is a great deal of intensity there, in the work and in the planning.

A MIDWEST ATHENS: THE NEW COLLEGE AT OAKLAND,
MICHIGAN

But I want now to turn to what seems to me in some ways more important for the general American scene, and that

is the effort to do something new in large public universities. Here I want to pick two institutions which seemed to
me, as I was considering this occasion, the most relevant
for the situation of York, because both are breakaway colleges of large existing universities which are trying to do
something different from the parent model. One is the new
college of Michigan State University in Oakland, which is
called for short MSUO; the other is the new college within
Wayne University in Detroit called Monteith College. Let
me give an all too abbreviated picture of each of these.
The first thing to be said about both institutions is that
they have departed from a growing pattern of establishing
an honours program within the great state universities;
these honours programs differ among themselves but typic-
ally give the run of the house, or special advanced sections,
to a few academically outstanding students, but ordinarily
without making any substantial changes in the university
structure itself. Both new Michigan institutions, in depart-
ing from the honours model, were founded with the idea of
accepting students that would be acceptable as regular—
not honours—students at the state university level. In
states like Michigan, both law and custom tend to channel
the better students to the state university with the poorer
going to the regional or local state institutions, sometimes
junior colleges and sometimes expanded former teachers
colleges.
The new college of Michigan State University in Oakland
is about thirty miles outside Detroit, and will accept
students in the top quarter of their high school class or
those who can furnish a somewhat equivalent record.[5] It
is at present largely non-residential, although small dormi-

[5]This selectivity might appear to make MSUO an honours college,
but the public high schools are of such varying calibre and the work
necessary to attain high grades in them is so frequently merely cursory,
that students can graduate in the top quarter of their class and still
be very poorly prepared for college not only by Ontario but also by
American standards.

tories are being built. It is primarily a commuter college for the area. In general, the commuter colleges, which educate so large a proportion of the college youth in America, seek to adapt themselves to local demands and to provide the sort of higher education that the local community considers relevant to its vocational and cultural ambitions. MSUO is experimental and indeed intrepid in its relatively unyielding resistance to local norms and definitions of what a college is. It has set its sights high, both in terms of academic demands and in terms of emphasizing liberal education as against direct vocational preparation (although such preparation in certain limited fields such as engineering and teaching is provided for).

Now in its third year, MSUO has an entering class of about 500; in comparison with state university behemoths, this is small. It is rigorous and despite its actual selectivity, there are a great many students who could not make the grade in some of the departments in the first years. The failure rate is not noticeably higher than at many state universities that use their entering year as a kind of screening, but the students in the community got the impression of an uncompromising institution with high standards that could not be bent to previous local norms. Some students have, in fact, withdrawn, declaring that they just don't want to work that hard for a degree and will go somewhere else. And as the college's standards have become better known, high school counsellors in the area have begun to channel to the college only students who they think have the capacity to stay the course.

I think I'm not being too unfair when I suggest that MSUO exists in an area that can boast of its automobiles— it is near Pontiac—but not of its high schools (though some of the latter are doing their best to meet the new challenge and opportunity). The youngsters come from working class and lower middle-class homes in which only a very

small proportion of the parents have had any college education or formal humanistic cultivation. Parents and children
have gained their idea of what a college is from the mass
media or from the more collegiate trappings of MSU
itself. But the new college makes no concessions to American popular culture or to the collegiate. There are no
fraternities; there are no extramural athletics; it is very
much the post-sputnik college without frills and tailfins. So
the students are suddenly presented with a very demanding,
a very unvocational, very humanistic program, which has
been adapted from the best Ivy League models—from
places like Columbia or Amherst—but not in any large
way compromised, and to a student body which, by Ivy
League definitions, is unselective and inexperienced in high
culture.

I was there several years ago when the humanities faculty
had just shown the movie *Henry V* and there was a great
deal of discussion of what the impact of this film had been
on the students. In the first place, many were unprepared
to see a Shakspeare movie. They didn't connect movies
with high culture. They didn't know what a Dauphin was;
they had all sorts of problems in following the movie. What
troubled sensitive faculty members even more was that
the film was work to the students. The students could be
led to high culture but they could not be led to enjoy it.
That was a two-generational step perhaps, not a one-genera-
tional step.

Indeed the faculty, when one talked with them, would
tell stories about an institution which had not yet developed
a student culture to protect the students from the faculty.
If a faculty member by mistake, let us say, should assign a
whole book of Plato rather than a half of a book for the next
period, the students would stay up all night and read it.
There was no communication among them that this was
illegitimate, that the faculty should be picketed or in other

ways sabotaged. They would obey, but that doesn't mean that they would enjoy it; they would do it: they were obedient.

Many on the faculty have a sense of mission at this institution based on whether they can keep it up. There are two problems in relation to the local community which are fighting issues. One is high standards, the resentment of the community at the rigour of the program, how hard their kids have to work and how many of them fail.[6] The students themselves have a great deal of pride about that: if they do not flunk out they feel challenged; they feel the program gives them a sense of adequacy, which is good.

The other issue, which has come up on several occasions, is academic freedom. Chancellor Varner of MSUO is alert enough to realize that if one gets a good faculty, one is likely to get one that can become something of an irritant to a conservative community. Prior to the election of 1960, an overwhelming majority of the MSUO faculty signed a public declaration in favour of candidate Kennedy—and this in a community that is violently divided between Walter Reuther of the United Auto Workers, locally identified with Kennedy and the Democratic party, and the auto magnates and "solid citizens" identified with the Republican party. About the same time, one of the professors created adverse local comment when he made a speech on Cuba deriding American policy. (I think it would have been perfectly acceptable in the *Globe and Mail*.) On the one hand, many faculty members coming from more protected institutions had not realized the intensity of local views

[6]Plans are now underway in Pontiac for a community junior college that will help relieve the pressure on MSUO. It should be added that the students themselves who have been flunked out of MSUO or who have voluntarily withdrawn apparently feel that they have had their fair chance and do not blame the institution. A good many, so far as I can discover continue their work for a degree at a less demanding institution.

(and perhaps the strength of anti-Reuther feeling), while on the other hand members of the business community, who had backed the new college financially and in other ways, had not realized what sort of commodity they were acquiring. The Chancellor had to try to educate the local community to see that it couldn't maintain a high-power institution without having academic freedom "problems" —at least in this time and at that place.

It would take us too far afield to seek to explore both the dangers and the protections provided for MSUO by its association with Michigan State University in East Lansing. The latter institution has, with great energy, been trying to "overtake and surpass" the older, more prestigeful and more academically reputable University of Michigan. This competition (into which Wayne State University in Detroit has entered more recently) has helped provide the setting for MSUO itself, giving it a certain support against possible resentments of faculty members at the parent institution who feel that the privileges and the publicity that have attended the new college are not the happiest commentary on their own —that is, the parent—institution.

GENERAL EDUCATION AT MONTEITH COLLEGE

The Monteith problem is a rather different one and the Monteith solution is a different one. In the first place, whereas Michigan State's new college is a full, four-year undergraduate college, Monteith College lives as part of Wayne—a big sprawling metropolitan university which is now part of Michigan's state university system. So students go to Monteith for approximately half the program and take the rest of the courses in their fields of concentration in Wayne. For instance, a student who is entering Wayne to go into engineering may choose Monteith, in which case he will get his first two years of General Education at Monteith, and he will get two upper-course, general programs, or colloquia, at Monteith.[7] But he will begin, certainly by his second year, to be taking civil engineering courses at Wayne as well; or indeed he might be in the Liberal Arts program at Wayne, let us say in Slavic studies, while also at Monteith. In other words, Monteith does not furnish the full complement of courses. It is as if York were saying to students in the upper-class years: "We can't give you a course in Chinese classics. You can concentrate on that at the University of Toronto, or wherever else you can find it in the area, but we will give you your General Education and your academic home." Thus Monteith does not have to start from scratch in quite the same way as MSUO for its total program.

I have the impression (not based on actual data) that the coming of MSUO opened the doors of college to some local residents who would otherwise not have considered going to college; one had to arrive on their doorstep for them to consider it as a possibility. Monteith, on the other hand, being part of an already existing university, tended to draw on those graduates of Detroit high schools who had already planned on attending college. Furthermore, some of the Detroit high schools are excellent. Monteith opened its doors to any student admitted to Wayne—in practice this has meant a B average in high school. In an effort to achieve a cross-section for purposes of comparative evaluation, Monteith sent invitations to every fifth student in some Wayne undergraduate colleges, or to every fourth or third in others. But since no students could be required

[7]Engineering students, however, are not required to take the natural science General Education sequence at Monteith. But a Monteith student planning to enter the College of Education or Law or Business Administration must take the three General Education sequences in the humanities, the social sciences, and the natural sciences, and if he wants a degree from Monteith, he must write a senior essay as well.

to enter Monteith and since Monteith did not reject those who voluntarily chose it, a certain selectivity could not be avoided even at the outset. At present, word has gotten around in Detroit that Monteith is different, more difficult than Wayne, and perhaps more radical and offbeat. Even after students have entered, a process of transfer continues between Wayne and its satellite institution, not always happily for Monteith's popularity within the parent institution.

OPPORTUNITY VERSUS DERACINATION

I have the sense that Monteith has a more adventurous student body, a more "hep" student body if you like. While I'm sure that there is a good deal of overlap between the average MSUO and the average Monteith student, the pacesetters at Monteith are very different; the student paper at Monteith, for instance, is a good deal more informal, not at all the "typical" college student paper, rather similar in some ways to York's MC^2—and I say this as a compliment to both. An active minority of Monteith students have formed a cohesive culture that gathers around the Student Centre, and this Student Centre is a hive of intellectual, musical, artistic activity and talk, even though Monteith, like MSUO, is a commuter college. One will find at Monteith what is far less likely at MSUO: students cutting classes in order to talk about ideas, or even not ideas, at the Student Centre. About 80 per cent of the students at both institutions are working at least part-time. This means that they are vulnerable to the recent depression in Michigan, and of course, as I have indicated, they are commuters. One could say that the intractable problems at both institutions arise from the fact that both make full-time intellectual and emotional demands on their students, while the latter are living in homes which (as I've said before) are not the sort of homes where it is taken for granted that a young person will attend college—where in fact even to find space and quiet in which to work while at home often constitutes a major problem.

Both institutions are very conscious of the difficulties their students face vis-à-vis their parents and their home communities. Thomas Wolfe wrote a book *You Can't Go Home Again* whose title has become a motto for many people who attend college. The forms in which the conflict arises, however, seem to me to differ at the two institutions. I shall try to illustrate the difference, perhaps unfairly and unrepresentatively, by an example taken from each.

I visited a class at MSUO in the Western Civilization course which everyone takes, and which is based on the Columbia General Education course and uses its syllabus. This particular week they were reading Luther's address to the Christian nobility of the German nation. This is a rip-roaring address full of religious and political dynamite. But the students appeared to be reading it as a text. I could see that some of the students were Lutheran, some were Catholic, some were Jewish. The teacher was a brilliant, magnetic man, excited by the material and eager to tell his students about the life of Luther and to put them back imaginatively into the time of Luther, pointing out, for example, that the church door where Luther posted his famous Theses was a bit like the notice board in the Student Centre. Even so, he was handling the address as a document, as a text, making no effort to relate their reading of it to their own religious experience or lack of it. He didn't raise the question for the Catholic students, for instance, as to whether they had heard anything about Luther from their priests, or ask the Presbyterian students if they had ever heard a predestinarian sermon. It may well be that he was wise to remain on the cognitive level, for the students, although a small class set up in the discussion mode, might not have been able to assimilate the issues when con-

fronted with them collectively. There is always the danger
of invading the students' privacy in such cases, and here
the focus on the text and on its mastery minimized that risk.

At the outset, thanks to the then Dean Robert Hoopes,
former professor of English, and the emphasis of the Western Civilization course, the dominant intellectual current at
MSUO seems to have been that of the humanities. In contrast to that, at Monteith for historical reasons the initial
leadership lay in the area of the social sciences, although
schematically the college grants equal hegemony to the
three staffs of social science, natural science, and humanities. Hence, my illustration from Monteith is picked from
the social science area. There during the election campaign
of 1960, the social science faculty had the students, every
one of them, take part in an election survey in the city of
Detroit; so that a Polish boy at Monteith, let us say—there
are many Poles in Detroit—would be encouraged to go and
sample voter attitudes towards the election in a Polish
neighbourhood. He might discover, for instance, that there
were many cross-pressures on Polish voters. If they were
Catholic, they might be drawn to Kennedy, but their dio-
cesan priest might be one of the many clerics who were opposed to Kennedy. Older voters might be hostile to the
young man and younger voters sympathetic. The students
would be made more aware of who they were; where they
come from; where they were going. Then they would go
back and discuss the Polish vote with students who had
done similar work in the Negro, the Italian, and all the
other bailiwicks of multi-ethnic Detroit.

It seems to me a fascinating question to ask which emphasis, that of Monteith or that of MSUO, will have most
impact on the complex triangular relationship of student,
faculty, and family. It seemed to me that a boy (or girl)
at MSUO who had been reading Luther's address to the
Christian nobility of the German nation was not likely to

go home to an automobile worker family and discuss it with them. On the one hand, he might regard himself as cut off from his parents by having read this order of material, but on the other hand this might make it easy for him to compartmentalize his college life and home life, keeping each in relative ignorance of the other, as he may have done earlier with conflicts between street and home and school and home. In contrast, the Monteith student who was engaged in an election survey could go home again in a new way, because after all his parents too were talking about the election. They could make statements about it, and he could say: "Oh yes, this is what such and such a family told me" or, "This is what happened when I went to that man's door and he turned the dog on me because he said all Wayne students are Communists." This kind of experience could be assimilated in the home, and the result might be that a student who was still living at home was not cut off from his parents in quite the same way that it seemed to me the MSUO students were, by being drawn into a general American highbrow culture with which their parents had for the most part no connection.

What interested me, in both these experiments, was the fact that large state institutions were not simply accreting more units and taking in the increasing numbers who want an education by extrapolation, by adding one more link to the endless chain, but by starting satellite institutions which had a different trajectory and a smaller humanly-scaled potentiality. The monolithic university model of the huge institutions—both the University of Michigan and Michigan State now have something like 25,000 students —was rejected in favour of institutions of more manageable size.

The problems that had not been solved at either of those institutions (or at the one or two California experiments of a similar sort: such as the new University of California branch at Riverside, California) are of course those that were indicated during my beginning remarks about the research orientation of the leading men.

FACULTY RECRUITMENT IN THE EXPERIMENTAL COLLEGE

Who is going to teach at an institution that is only an undergraduate college and one that is engaged in experimentation, which means more committee meetings, more work, more face-to-face dealings with students? The answer that I myself give to this question—which is the question all undergraduate colleges seem to me to face—is that it can only be solved by enormous amounts of financial support and freedom in such institutions. I am convinced, for instance, that faculty members who teach in an institution which has no university attached to it, no graduate school, no research facilities, should have a Sabbatical leave every three years during which they can go to another university and work full time there, to feel they are keeping up in their field, to feel that they are not losing their mobility, and can come back refreshed for the arduous work of undergraduate teaching.[8] It seems to me that some such arrangement as this is essential if the small institution is to survive.

One has to give the academic man who devotes himself to undergraduates, which is regarded as an unprofessional pursuit, this kind of professional opportunity. But one has

[8]Initial experience with a comparable plan at Wesleyan University raises difficult practical issues of maintaining continuity for study in a small department where the absence of a single man may mean there are no courses left to take in one's upper-class years and may also mean a serious diminution of colleagueship for the remaining one or more faculty members in the department. I would like to see an experiment tried in which, for instance, three faculty members took a group of Sophomores and carried them through their senior year in a particular and hopefully novel grouping of specialities; at the end of this time, the trio might dissolve, one or more members going on leave and any others free to join some other fluid grouping, or to work with freshmen, thus not establishing a formal departmental institution that needs permanent or near-permanent vestal care.

to do more than that. One has to ask oneself questions about what it is that the undergraduate professor wants to do with the young men and women whose education he helps to supervise. And it seems to me that the dangers I have indicated looming ahead of us are not the dangers that most academicians are still contending against: of slackness, of indolence, of anti-intellectualism. These dangers are certainly present but they are being rapidly overcome. The danger that I see ahead of us is that of the ambivalent but weighty impact of donnish professors who cannot communicate with students who are not going to be like them; who are going to do other things, who are going to go into other careers.

I was telling several newspaper and C.B.C. people at lunch about a former student of mine who started graduate work at L.S.E. and then left it to go into journalism, and how most of my colleagues, who considered him a bright and promising student, regretted this because he wasn't going to become like them. It seemed to me that this was a kind of provinciality on their part, in their assumption that only in academies can the intellectual life be led; whereas I am convinced that the intellectual life flourishes and suffers in many different professions and ways of life, and that there is no necessary connection between being an intellectual and being an academic man. Plainly, I didn't feel this man was lost to scholarship by entering journalism, and I don't view students as manpower for the cold war; nor do I view them as manpower for social science, nor for any particular field of work or style of life. In a hopefully yet insufficiently free society, in a rich society, the only people who can decide what that society needs are the young people themselves. The best that we can do as teachers is to help them develop along the lines in which they would tend to grow if growth were their aim.

It seems to me to the credit of both MSUO and Monteith that a large proportion of their faculties is prepared to work with students who are most unlikely to enter academic life, and who will only in a few cases have the resources or opportunities to enter any of the traditionally free professions. With varying emphases at the two colleges, there is hope on the part of the faculties that the college experience will illuminate in a general, truly liberal, way later non-professional, non-academic life. At their best, I believe, it is not a division of society into intellectuals and into non-intellectuals that these faculty members seek, but rather a society in which everyone is in some measure an intellectual, enabled by his college education to go on making sense of his experience and enriched by the recorded experience of other places and times.

With that, I would like to draw these formal remarks to a close and turn to questions from the audience.

THE LOCATION OF GENERAL EDUCATION

Question:

For a point of clarification: In the second experiment that you describe, in which general education was left to the fourth year, what exactly happened the first three years?

Answer:

We deal here with a plan which has not yet been spelled out, let alone put into practice. I believe it is planned that in the first three years people will concentrate in their majors, beginning with the freshman year. Would they be able to switch majors? I can't say as to that. I believe they might be able to within the limits of the department's requirements. Actually, this problem exists in a different form already at Harvard and many other institutions, thanks to the so-called Advanced Standing Program. An increasing number of students are entering the leading institutions as sophomores on the basis of their high school records, which means that they must enter in a field, and they must decide in advance what their field is. Your question has the implication, if I understood you, which I think is the correct one; namely, if the student already in high school got a very narrow view of the academic map, and simply continues this in his college career, he may spend three years in the Bowdoin plan in something which he wouldn't want to do if he had more opportunity to look around. It seems to me that this is part of a more general problem of our life, which might be called the problem of consumer research in the institutions into which one is going. We have excellent consumer research on consumer goods; we have very inadequate consumer research on educational goods. Thus a person, in the first place, goes to a college which may not be the best one for him or her; in the second place, he goes into a field or a major which may not be the best for him—in each case, with terribly little knowledge of what he is doing. Now, one purpose of freshman year general education is to give a wider orientation to the fields of knowledge, and this is, of course, one of the things which is held against the plan of postponing general education to the fourth year.

Question:
   One of the gentlemen on the platform with you has decried the professional school for its lack of attention to academica. Do you feel that the type of education you have described at some of these colleges, such as Monteith, would be preferable to the professional school, or does the special school man have no place in one of these institutions?

Answer:
   You mean a man who is going on to professional school? You mean a man who is going into medicine, law or engineering? I will repeat the question. President Ross, presumably, in his book has decried the professionalism or

vocationalism of the professional school: in the kinds of institutions I have been discussing, does the man who is going on into a professional school need this kind of general education as a precursor to his professional training? One of the answers to this is an empirical one. If one asks whence, within Wayne University, came the support for starting a new institution which would compete with the existing Wayne Liberal Arts College, the answer is it came from certain of the professional schools (the medical school, the engineering school, the law school, the social work school) whose officers wanted undergraduates who had not specialized and who were more awakened, more eman- cipated intellectually, than those who had regarded them- selves as going into these fields from early college training on. I have felt in talking to professional school faculty members that they are increasingly searching for the under- graduate who has not prepared himself by doing the things which he will have to do over again in the professional school.

In contrast, I can quote to you a conversation I had with a psychologist colleague who was insisting that he preferred to take into the graduate psychology department people who had done psychology as undergraduates. I said to him: "Look here, there isn't that much psychology to spend eight years on it. If they learned it in a good college, like Swarth- more let us say, what will you teach them?" He said: "The point is that I don't want to teach them. I want to use them as apprentices from the very beginning." It seems to me that this is an unwarranted desire; it is not primarily a peda- gogic but a somewhat exploitative desire. It may be useful for the student to be an apprentice. It gets him closer to the faculty than he would otherwise get, but it is not the way to set up a curriculum. Such remarks only confirm my impression that in most fields there is no need for under- graduate specialization in what one will do later. I am inclined to think that there is no field which an able student cannot enter at a professional school level with not much more than one year's additional preparation.

Professor Robert Knapp at Wesleyan and some foundation officials in the States have raised the possibility of creating a one-year moratorium in which a person, concentrating in classics for example, and now wanting to go to medical school, can take that minimum of biological sciences or mathematics which he needs. I don't think that it would often take more than a year. I think if one looks at the matter institutionally, what one sees is this: the more prestigeful the field, the more sought after it is, the earlier into childhood it can force the point of no return. This says a great deal about its power and nothing whatsoever about its substance.

WASTE AND THE DROPOUT

Question:

Isn't there any concern on the Oakland campus among the faculty about the very large dropoff of students?—you mentioned 40 per cent, a tremendous wastage.

Answer:

I'm afraid I didn't make myself clear here: while there are departments which in a particular term fail perhaps as many as 40 per cent in a particular examination, over-all the percentage of dropouts is now—I'm told—averaging around 5 or 6 per cent per year or an over-all attrition in the course of a four-year program of 20 to 25 per cent. In terms of American norms and especially state university norms, this not particularly high. What *is* different at MSUO is the fact that students cannot avoid taking difficult courses in the liberal arts and sciences, by hiding out academically, as it were, in more or less vocational or pre-professional undergraduate courses; and this explains the high rate of failure in some of the science and other courses that have occasioned anguish for both faculty and students.

I might add that two attitudes seem to compete with
others among faculty members at MSUO about all this. On
the one hand, there is the fear that students who are found
not to be worthy of going on at MSUO will be damaged,
and the departments may seek to define their educational
standing vis-à-vis each other by insisting on their severity
and rigour under the name of "high standards." In consequence, there is a great effort, possible in the small college
with small classes, to work individually with students who
are serious and who want to learn but who are having
trouble, whether owing to inadequate abilities or inadequate
preparation; and when such students must be let go, there
is an effort to make the transition for them to a less demanding setting in a fashion that is compassionate rather than
ruthless. But on the other side, it is difficult to understand
the energy and determination with which many faculty
members hold to their high standards, and may appear to
be more punitive to students than in fact they are or would
like to be, without seeing this effort as part of the general
onslaught of the intellectual against American mass culture.
That is, the Oakland faculty member who is failing his
students and who may be saying, without dishonesty, that
it hurts him more than it hurts them, is telling himself he
is fighting for high standards in an affluent, fat, slobby
society. He is saying he is taking the Kennedy, patrician,
ascetic line, if you like, in academic life; and I think one
should see it as part of this cultural onslaught against the
slackness of the affluent society. This is a faculty some of
whom are proud of not owning a television set, proud of
having foreign cars, proud of their modern art—men who
would love to have the modern art which is a glory of York
as I have seen it here in this building. Such a faculty feels
that it is crusading for all that is noble and high and elevated
in American life against its flabbiness and indolence. If
President Kennedy has a physical fitness campaign, this is

an intellectual fitness campaign. I think if one doesn't see it in that Marine combat context, one cannot understand it.

Then one would ask subsidiary questions about which, to my regret, nothing seems to be known, or almost nothing. There is a chapter by Vice-President John Summerskill of Cornell in the book *The American College*, edited by R. Nevitt Sanford, which has just come out, in which he talks about dropouts. This is the first serious study that I have known of what happens. I have some skepticism about the term "wastage" that is used. One could say that this experience might be creative for the people who had it even if it didn't go on for four years. The questions are: How do they interpret it? What do they do next? Do they go somewhere else to continue their education? Do they become anti-intellectual because they are sore at how they were treated? Do they form active cadres of the John Birch society to get the "Reds" out of the university? Very little is known, I think, about the dropouts.

Moreover, as already suggested, one has to see what MSUO is doing in terms of the practice of the state universities of the Middle West. The way they have dealt with equality of opportunity has been to say, "We will take all comers but we won't keep them all"; and to use the freshman year as a kind of long-run expensive and traumatic College Board exam. It is wasteful in some ways but whether it is as wasteful as people often believe would have to be shown, I think. This I suggest as a research project for those who would like to see what really happens to these young people.

THE DIALECTIC OF DEMAND

Question:

Do you mean to suggest that the professor shouldn't teach what he wants to teach but what the students want to learn?

Answer:

This really takes us into a very searching, important, essential area in talking about education. I think that the student and the professor both come to the encounter with vested interests, neither of which can be trusted. The professor has the vested interests of his discipline, and he is often aware of the audience of his colleagues as well as the audience in front of him. Indeed, in a staff-taught course such as I have participated in at Chicago and Harvard, one is faced at the same time with both audiences. For further illustration, let me turn to the class I attended at MSUO on the address of Luther. Suppose this had been what I don't believe it was; namely, a virtuoso performance put on for the benefit of the visiting firemen or for the benefit of other colleagues, and to use a phrase of Veblen, not with "an eye single" for the students in the class at the moment. Even so, the students might well have gained more than they would have from a discussion premised on what they themselves were aware that they wanted to learn about. I doubt if the students themselves would have known that it would profit them to read Luther's address to the nobility or anything of the sort. The students, after all, come with their parochialisms and with their frozen definitions of who they are, what they can do, and what they can't do. One of the jobs of the teacher is to help the students, as I am trying to help you here, not to be afraid to be ridiculous. It seems to me that you can't get educated if you are afraid to be ridiculous. The professor's job is to help the student to learn that he can be ridiculous and that it isn't fatal, that he can open himself up in areas where he is not competent.

Let me illustrate exactly what I mean from the area of vocational guidance. It often happens that a student will come to college and say: "I have taken a test and the test says (let us say) that I will make a good accountant. I have these and these profiles on my test scores which resemble the inventories of successful accountants. The test shows that I will not make—what was a minor interest of mine in high school—I will not make a good journalist. I lack these and these abilties of the good journalist, the extroversion or whatever." Now, in the first place, if one looks at the test and studies it, one sees that any judgment that this boy will make a good accountant is the judgment that he is like the accountants who are now accountants. This doesn't mean that he will make a good accountant because accountancy may be different when he is through, or he may make it different. In the second place, it leaves out entirely the individual elements of temperament and gift. It may be that this boy's uncle is an accountant, and this is a reason for him not to be an accountant, and yet one of the reasons why he feels some pressure or desire to enter the field. It may be that he will do very good work in a field which is not, by the test, defined as his best, but in which nevertheless he feels some sense of excitement and to which he is drawn. The tests may put him off from it. Now the same is true of a student choosing his fare in college. You will often find a student who says, "Well I can't do history—I never did well in history." It turns out that what he means by "I never did well in history" is "I didn't get A's in history the way I did in geology or mathematics or French." That doesn't mean that he didn't do well in history by national norms. It doesn't mean that he couldn't become an eminent historian. This is the kind of thing that the student doesn't know, that the faculty collectively might know a little less badly than he, and he can be helped by exposing himself in a way that he wouldn't like to do; but he needs to be supported while he is doing it. To repeat: it seems to me that the task of the faculty—and here the questioner is quite right —is not to teach the student what he comes wanting to learn, but also not to create disciples for itself in its specialty, but rather to see what this student might become if he were less frightened of failing in areas which are not his optimal areas by previous definition or experience. Thereby he creates a new sense of himself—that is the student's self —as he goes on with his education. This is an encounter. This is a process of give-and-take between faculty and student, in which where the student is, and where the faculty member is, are both important but neither are end points.

THE MORATORIUM

Question:

Could one achieve the same thing by a student staying out of school for a year?

Answer:

Where would you locate the year? Between high school and college or one of the college years? The result will not be the same, but I think there is much to be said for such interim years. Harvard has shown itself increasingly lenient: as its standards have risen, its retention rate has also risen by virtue of letting or encouraging its students to take years off without requiring that they bring anything back in the way of worthwhile pieces of paper. They can drive a truck, or bum around or whatever, and come back and they will be welcome. This is an increasing phenomenon among the boys. What this reflects, it seems to me, are two things. One is the meritocratic pressures I have already referred to; that is, the highly prepared—even over-prepared—boys who come in drilled to take examinations, who then suddenly wonder what this is all about, this endless escalator on which they are working. They then conclude that college isn't life; so they seek life in California, or New York, or on a boat or something; and then they decide college is not so bad after all. They come back with less illusions that life is life-like and more sense of why they are in college. Many experiences of this sort have encouraged the administration to be relaxed about this phenomenon.

One of the things that puzzles and interests me is that the girls don't do this, although the girls are, if anything, more driven even than the boys, and submit to a more rigorously academic hegemony over their lives. There are several reasons why the girls don't do it. One is that increasingly they feel that they must get their A.B. before they get married, and they therefore can't afford to waste a year which will make them old, maybe as "old" as 23 or 24, by the time they leave college. In the second place, families still are more protective towards women, and colleges are more protective of women, so that a girl can't hitch-hike around the country and get a job as a dishwasher with the same relative sanguinity from parents and other people *in loco parentis* that a boy can. I think that discrimination, often quite subtle, against women as professors and students remains the great Jim Crow of our liberal academic life.

MSUO: PROBLEMATIC TRAJECTORIES

Question:

I was wondering about the continuing effects of Oakland on the various students prior to entering a college. Would you say these are students from a rather low-calibre high school and community in general? What would be the effect of Oakland on them? And what is the effect of Oakland on the students after they leave the college there in their further university life, whether it be undergraduate or graduate?

Answer:

In the first place, the high schools in the area are now under some pressure to improve, and MSUO people appear themselves engaged in facilitating that improvement where they can. Consequently the enormous gap that, in my judgment, at present separates MSUO from its surrounding high schools may become somewhat narrowed. In the second place, the effect on the trajectory of the students who come out of these high schools and this cultural background into the highly intense Oakland academic atmosphere isn't known yet, since the third class is only now there. There aren't any graduates. I am very puzzled, as I have implied in my reference to the possible deracination, as to what some of the consequences will turn out to be. In any situation of cultural change through which an individual passes, it is hard to separate opportunities and accomplishments from risk and suffering. One can't help asking—and perhaps this was in your mind—given the unselective character of the homes from which the students come, and given the highly academic and exciting and demanding fare to which they are exposed at MSUO, what will become of them? Where will society use them since they have no backing, they have no sponsorship? Certainly some will go on to graduate school who would never have thought before Oakland appeared they would go to college at all. Their case is clear, they will go to graduate school. Others will go into secondary high school teaching; this is clear. Some will take a fifth year to become engineers, and will presumably be more in demand than engineers out of the straight engineering course. But what will happen to the total community, I don't know. I'm sure that many in the administration and faculty at MSUO are deeply concerned with this question.

CYNICISM OR DETACHMENT IN COMPARATIVE PERSPECTIVE?

Question:

Many of your terms are unfamiliar. We are not used to taking students as commodities, and universities as packages, and so on. I was wondering if you would just say a few words on this interesting metaphor?

Answer:

The question was an ironical one and I appreciate it. I think what I would say about the metaphor is along this line—a great deal could be said about it. In the two days I have spent in Toronto, which of course are traveller's licence, I have had the feeling that in Canada higher education is a pretty sacred thing and that to look realistically at universities, as one looks at other institutions, is not a customary thing. I think one understands institutions better if one sees them comparatively, if one sees them as processes, and if one sees the cycle of human life—as my former colleague, and a man from whom I learned much on these matters, Everett Hughes, has often said—as a series of contiguous cycles and turning points of men and institutions who are engaged in separate trajectories and contingencies which come together at focal points. The danger, I think, of this kind of view is obvious. It is the danger of cynicism, or nihilism; of being thought to debunk the motives and ideals which create such a hall as we are in, or such an occasion as we are engaged in. I feel always that I tread very narrow lines in what I say and what I write and what I do when I study universities. I am sometimes unhappy about what I have written on the subject—I do go back and read it. I feel that I have underplayed the idealism and I have overplayed the opportunism, or vested-interest elements in academic, as in any other human, enterprise. I feel this especially when the tide turns my way; that is, when education or certain institutions are no longer viewed as different from others, and when cynicism, beat attitudes, and withdrawal begin to be prevalent among the young.

Let me illustrate some of the reasons why I use the semantics about universities that I do, although it may be inappropriate to this audience with which I am not familiar, whereas it would be appropriate with audiences with which I am familiar. In the ten or fifteen years in the better

American colleges there has been a continuation of a process, which began thirty years ago, of revulsion against business careers by the most gifted and sensitive young people. Most of the students that I have had at Chicago or Hopkins or Harvard have thought business was for Philistines, and that they could only make for themselves a version of the intellectual life in academic life itself. I sometimes feel when I look at a group of my students, and this is an unselected group—I am not talking about students who come to me for a special subject—that half of them want my job and the other half are going into psychiatry! As I have watched this depreciation of business develop, assisted by such books as *The Organization Man*, or the writings of Vance Packard, and the general way in which people talk about business careers in the American intellectual life, I have been deeply troubled because I have felt two illusions were being created. One was the illusion that business is a field in which one could only have a dull and complacent, if secure and well-paid life, and this is one of the self-confirming prophecies. I would say that, on the whole, hardly any Harvard students of quality go to the Business School. The Harvard undergraduate at the Harvard Business School is a rarity, and he is likely to come from the lower parts of the class, if he can get into the Business School from that jumping-off place. And I think this is helping to create an image of business leadership which then may become self-confirming and which is an injustice to what is possible in a business career; that is, to its intellectual possibilities, its adventurous possibilities. But the converse illusion seems to me no less dangerous; namely, that academic life is not a business, that there are no business or commercial elements in the professions. When these elements are discovered, then cynicism and disillusion beset those people who thought they had escaped commercialism by entering an academic career. When they see, "Ah yes, here is human nature again, here are vested interests," then their resignation from the human lot is likely to be total. This is why I try to take this comparative perspective, to look across national boundaries too. Had there been time tonight, I would have talked about my recent study of Japanese universities and how they are similar and how they are different from the American or Canadian ones. In this effort at comparison the hope is, the aim is—and it often misfires—that people will emerge more amused by the human experience, more, if you like, ironical, more detached, but also less likely to be either greatly illusioned or greatly disillusioned or cynical.

On Creativity

Robert Ulich

Robert Ulich

Robert Ulich is the James Bryan Conant Professor of Education Emeritus, Harvard University. Born in Bavaria and educated in European universities, Professor Ulich became Counsellor in charge of higher education in the Saxon Ministry of Education and Professor at the Technological University of Dresden before joining the faculty of Harvard in 1934. At Harvard, he was Professor of Education, and also taught in the Department of History of Science and Learning, and in the Divinity School. His main interests are in the history and philosophy of education and in comparative education. He is the author of numerous articles and books that have been widely translated. Some of his better known works are History of Educational Thought, The Human Career: A Philosophy of Self-Transcendence, *and* The Education of Nations.

'Tis to create, and in creating live
A being more intense. . . .
BYRON

WHAT is creativity? It is an act that changes the environment of man for the better, that pushes one or several persons ahead, that produces more favourable conditions for humanity, or that deepens our insight into ourselves while it widens our intellectual horizon. It gives a person the feeling of transcending his ordinary limitations for a worthwhile purpose; it engenders a sense of heightened self-confidence and of justified pride. Thus creativity has its reward in itself, however much we all hope that our endeavours find also some external recognition.

In some way, every normal individual has felt the joys and pangs of creativity. But we might understand the process better if we concentrate first on the work of outstanding men, say of genius, though in not too strict a sense. Our word "genius" is itself related to a Latin and ultimately Indo-Germanic root which means "to produce" or "to beget." Furthermore, our understanding may be improved if we reflect for a while on the nature of seemingly opposite forms of creativity, that of the scientist and that of the artist.

THE DIFFERENCE AND SIMILARITY IN SCIENTIFIC AND
ARTISTIC CREATIVITY

The Accumulative Quality of Science
When we contemplate the development of science, especially that of the physical sciences, we envisage an accumulative process, both in terms of knowledge and in terms of participants. Probably 90 per cent of the scientists whom humanity has produced are alive today and work in enormous organizations with world-wide contacts. Rapidly more and more previously hidden data become known. They are

examined under new combinations and particularly with the help of refined experiments, and every generation of scientists must hope that its disciples will improve its findings, perhaps even by disprovement. It is likely that, if one man had not made a specific discovery, another man would have made it. Many great inventions have been made almost simultaneously, not only by two, but even by three persons.

In contrast, we have not the impression of accumulation and simultaneousness when we think of a sculpture of Michelangelo or a symphony of Beethoven. For these works convey to us a sense of uniqueness, perhaps a sense of loneliness, and—to a high degree at least—a sense of perfection. We dare not "improve" a true work of art, be it even a small poem. Neither bigness nor smallness matters—there it is. We can only imitate it.

Obedience to Reality

At the beginning of the philosophy of modern science, Francis Bacon wrote the following words in his *Novum Organum*:

Man, as the minister and interpreter of Nature, does and understands as much as his observations on the order of Nature, either with regard to things or to mind, permit him, and neither thinks nor is capable of more. . . . Knowledge and human power are synonymous, since the ignorance of the cause frustrates the effect. For Nature is only subdued by submission, and that which in contemplative philosophy corresponds with the cause, in practical science becomes the rule.

These sentences would not have become so famous, had they not expressed an essential element in the scientist's work. Whether we call it "submission to Nature," as Bacon did, or call it respect for reality, the scientist's discipline consists in patient observation, repeated experimentation, untiring trial and error, and renunciation of subjectivity to achieve the highest possible degree of objectivity.

In contrast, the artist appears to us as a symbol of freedom. He is permitted to be and to assert himself, to cultivate his subtlest and most intimate feelings, and to transform the world, instead of submitting to it. He should tell us of the heights and depths of his existence in order to show us Nature as it is within us, and if he shows us Nature as it is without us, it is not the Nature of the scientist. One need only compare the descriptions of a thunderstorm by a poet and a physicist. The artist, furthermore, does not need a laboratory; he is himself one.

Causality
The scientist stands before a world of majestic greatness, but nevertheless a world determined by laws, a world full of mysteries, but not of miracles, a world deaf and silent to our ardent prayers. If we discover the forces working in cancer, we can conquer them. If we do not, they will continue to destroy both young and old, including the finest flowers of humanity. There is neither rationality nor irrationality, neither kindness nor cruelty, in this world of Nature. It is below, or, if you want, above these human categories. The scientist, qua scientist, should not project his sentiments into the object of his research. Because the scholars humanized Nature in the Middle Ages, they limited their ability to understand it. But we have no objection if the artist allows God or the devil, human impulses or human lethargies, to intervene with life. Even the rationalists of the eighteenth century spoke of "Nature and of Nature's God."

Intuition
When discussing the differences in the creativity of the scientist and the artist, one can hardly forget the phenomenon of intuition. For a long time scientifically oriented psychologists have shied away from this confusing concept.

Indeed, there is hardly a more elusive mental act than that sudden flash of insight piercing the foggy horizons of the mind. Yet, the fact that something defies explanation is inadequate evidence for negating its existence.

Now, as new psychological concepts and methods emerge, intuition is also receiving attention.[1]

Intuition is defined in our dictionaries as a form of immediate cognition obtained without recourse to inferential and sequential reasoning. This is, of course, no explanation; it is not even a description. For how can one arrive at any communicable statement without some kind of sequential reasoning?

But whether or not we use the term intuition, we are aware of a power in the human mind, which in contrast to the more pedestrian procedure of ordinary thinking and concluding leaps, as it were, immediately into the centre of a problem. One might envisage two archers. One makes first a number of trial shots in order to approach the goal, the other plays for a while with bow and arrow, then draws, and after shooting almost aimlessly, hits the bull's eye. Common opinions suggest that the scientist must proceed through trials, whereas the artist is the diviner. Perhaps, so some of the more arrogant type may believe, if they had been trained long enough and had been confronted with the same configuration of facts and problems in a good laboratory, they too might have made the famous discovery.

But our admiration of the work of an artistic genius, or our appreciation of one of the simple yet beautiful folk melodies that have enriched the life of every nation, is not accompanied by the assumption that we also could have created these with adequate training.

There is something beyond effort. And this, so it seems

[1]See Jerome S. Bruner, *The Process of Education* (Harvard University Press, 1960) and Robert Ulich, *The Human Career: A Philosophy of Self-Transcendence* (New York: Harper and Brothers, 1956).

to us, is the grace reserved for the artist by some heavenly constellation, or by the "muses." Around him mythology has wound a wreath of garlands. One need only remember the legend of Vergil in the Christian Middle Ages for a classical example. Mythology has neglected the scientist, unless one takes the Prometheus myth as the beginning of man's poetry about science and technology.

Yet the dichotomy between scientific and artistic processes of creativity is not as wide as we believe. They are not mutually exclusive, but interrelated expressions of the same urge to transform mental perceptions into symbols and images. Our failure to see their common root is the result partly of our intellectual and our cultural tradition.

For the appreciation of the aesthetic quality of science one must have been trained in the art of creative seeing; i.e., one must have learned to recognize the beauty in a creation which is outside the realm of the conventional, such as a scientific model, a mathematical arrangement, or a machine designed to vigorous standards of function.

Furthermore, our freedom of judgment suffers from old social prejudices. In the older privileged groups of our society, aesthetic values were given priority over what were called the utilitarian values, though the former may have allowed the artist to starve and the peasant to be exploited. Old aristocrats collected art and some gentlemen even aspired to make their lives and personalities works of art.

On the other hand, science owes its rise and prestige largely to the middle class. Yet, despite its revolutionary spirit in economics and politics, this middle class preserved and even refined the genteel values of the feudal class. Only more recently has a kind of literature been more widely appreciated which reveals the relation between science and beauty, the fascination in the personality of an inventor, and the union between a bridge and the surrounding landscape. The old master-builders and gardeners, however, always wanted their work to be regarded as an encomium of Nature. Indeed, the decorative urge of mankind has exerted itself just as long and devotedly in man's daily instruments as in special works of art. Only when the artist became separated from the guildsman and signed his work by name was art alienated from the collective genius of mankind.

In order to prove the artificiality of the rigid dichotomy betwen the scientific and the artistic genius, let us reconsider the characteristics we attributed to the scientist's work.

Certainly the *accumulative* quality in science is evident by the fact that calculus would have been invented without Newton and Leibniz and the idea of evolution eventually would have been transferred from an old philosophical intuition to a scientific hypothesis if Darwin had not existed. Nevertheless, each of these men made "the leap" from the unknown to the known as an individual, unaware that someone else struggled with the same problem. Also in them was something of the singleness and solitude of the artist.

On the other hand, to a degree at least, art also is accumulative. The portrait and the perspective of the Renaissance did not appear suddenly, nor did counterpoint in music. Clearly the development of architecture is the history of an amazing continuity in the accumulation of experience.

Also in relation to the second characteristic of science, its "obedience to reality," the contrast to art is easily exaggerated. If Bacon's advice to the scientist, "submit, obey, and use only the inductive method," had been closely followed, he would have deprived science of its imaginative quality and thus retarded its progress. Perhaps it is science that has built the most daring superstructure over and above the structure of reality. This edifice has been erected with the help of mathematical symbols which certainly are not inherent in Nature as such, but are products of the human mind just as much as poetic and religious symbols, though of a different kind.

On the other hand, the artist also cannot work without submission to reality. Where can one find more realistic piety than in the praying hands drawn by Dürer and in those sculptured by Rodin? And unconventional though the life of some artists may have been, when they disregarded the discipline, asceticism and obedience which their work demanded, their genius left them. In his memoirs, *Dichtung und Wahrheit*, Goethe speaks with admiration of the German poet, Johann Christian Günther, who lived two generations before him. But he concludes the description of the poet's personality and work with the memorable words: "He did not know how to discipline himself and thus he dissipated his life and his poetic talent." (Er wusste sich nicht zu zähmen und so zerrann ihm sein Leben wie sein Dichten.)

These remarks about submission to reality introduce our third characteristic of the scientist's productivity, his confrontation with a world of *causality*. By no means is his mind a mere reflection of the apparent rigidity we suppose to exist in the laws of Nature. He has the freedom to look or not to look at a particular section of the cosmos; he can look at it from different angles and he can choose different interpretations. To a degree, his choice depends on his personality. Every great scientist had not only an experimental and analytical, but also a speculative, bent. Such men as Kepler, Swedenborg, Fechner and Faraday were mystics, more so than many poets. Bacon himself saw no contrast between his *Instauratio Magna* and his *Meditationes Sacrae*.

On the other hand, the work of art also has its inner causality, or what we may call its "truth." We have schools of naturalism or realism, represented by men like Zola and Maupassant who were better psychologists and sociologists than many writers of academic textbooks. Indeed, every great novelist is both a master of fiction and an observer of life. In every work of art, even in the most subjective poem, we demand an inner order, unless the author expressly declares himself a "Dadaist" or whatever name he may give himself. Many a troubled person takes refuge in an aesthetic creation because he finds there a coherence and continuum of meaning and inner rhythm which he has lost in himself and the seemingly cruel world of humanity. And since the time of Pythagoras men have speculated about the affinity between music and mathematics.

Finally, we referred to *intuition* as a concept for distinguishing between the scientific and the artistic talent. Certainly, artists have affirmed the effect of intuition more often than scientists, partly because they are highly self-conscious, and partly because there is a highly intuitive element in art. But mathematicians and scientists have also acknowledged the relation between their discoveries and this gift.

In his book, *The Way of an Investigator*,[2] the famous physiologist Walter Bradford Cannon includes a chapter on the "Role of Hunches" in which he speaks of the somewhat irrational behaviour of scientific creativity. Ideas come when one wakes up from sleep; there occurs "the unearned assistance of sudden and unpredicted insight," and wakefulness at night, "though unwelcome, can be a source of new and better ideas." . . . "I have long trusted," Professor Cannon confesses, "unconscious processes to serve me." Besides referring to testimonies of Helmholtz and other great scientists, he quotes Darwin's autobiographical report on the sudden synthesis of "the great number of facts" without "general meaning" from which the idea of evolution arose. "I can remember the very spot in the road, whilst in my carriage, when to my joy, the solution occurred to me."

[2]Walter Bradford Cannon, *The Way of an Investigator: A Scientist's Experience in Medical Research* (New York: W. W. Norton, 1945).

The similarity between scientific and artistic creativity becomes all the more evident when we read how artists, who at the same time emphasize the value of intuition, proclaim also the afflictions, the pains of craftsmanship, the impersonality, and the slow and constantly self-correcting process of their work. In Thomas Mann's short novel *Tonio Kröger* the author derides the sentimentalist who believes that the poet has just to follow his emotions in order to create his work. On the contrary, so Tonio Kröger says, the poet must first put his sentiments "on ice"; he has to "observe, comprehend and systematize even the most tortuous," and he has to go through the "nausea of radical truth" (Erkenntnisekel) before he becomes mature. Creative art is for Tonio Kröger, as for many writers, a kind of sickness. Loneliness and asceticism are the conditions of success. We may also listen to the sad statement of Henry James: "We work in the dark, we do what we can, our doubt is our passion and our passion is our task. The rest is the madness of art."

After this comparison between scientific and artistic creativeness we can now state the differences, but also the similarities, in the scientific and the artistic processes. The scientist, more than the artist, operates within a steadily developing continuum of knowledge. He is more indebted to his predecessors, more dependent on observation of existing, though perhaps still hidden, data, and more forced to submission. He is more outer-directed; the artist is more inner-directed. The scientist must attempt to interpret the causality inherent in a given reality, whereas the artist creates causality within an autonomous fictitious setting. The concept of intuition will be discussed differently among scientists and artists.

Yet, the lines of distinction are oscillating. The intuitive factor plays a role in both areas. There is an artistic element also in scientific creativeness. Some scientists are masters of style. Of the brothers William and Henry James it has been said that the first was perhaps the greater poet and the second the greater scientist.

Despite its wondrous variety, mental creativity flows from the same source; i.e., the power of man to transform his experiences into ideas by means of setting intervals of informative reflection between his first impulsive reaction to a problem and his final answer. Philosophy tells us about the criteria we should follow on the way from impulse to disciplined thinking: relevance, analysis, synthesis and exclusion of otherness, consistency, compatibility, and universality. These criteria apply also to the artist. And although the vision of truth on the scientist's horizon is different from the truth of the artist, we also expect some kind of truth from him. Both are enemies of chaos and searching for form and Gestalt.

Moreover we may refer to large areas on the *globus intellectualis* that lie between what, for the sake of brevity, we called science and art. The humanities, from philosophy and history to philology (unless it is pure linguistics), require minds equally open to the demands of strict scholarly discipline and the demands of aesthetic sensibility. New and rapidly expanding departments have invaded the academic arena which, since Heinrich Rickert's books on the differences between the sciences of culture and the science of Nature, are still struggling for methodological clarification, such as anthropology, psychology, sociology and education. Certainly, there is need for science in these new branches of knowledge. But they become barren whenever, impressed by the results of the quantitative and non-evaluative aspects of their disciplines, they eliminate the aesthetic and valuative element.

Ultimately, the mind is one, though its creative energy flows through many channels. Some very rare geniuses, such as Leonardo, Michelangelo and Goethe, were both artists and scientists. Why one faculty prevails over the other in most men of high talent we do not know. Perhaps we would be wiser if we knew what kind of psycho-physical conditions, partly hereditary and partly acquired, are necessary to produce an investigator of the forces and forms of Nature and those essential to producing a creator to whom the world speaks through sound and rhythm. But we will have to wait, and the full answer may never be given.

PSYCHOLOGY AND CREATIVITY

The ultimate oneness of creative minds becomes evident also when we try to determine the type of person and the typical attitudes most conducive to creativity.

The most recent investigations[3] reveal that creative persons, whether scientific or artistic, have the gifts we generally relate to productive intelligence. They are open-minded, curious, searching, never satisfied with the given but challenged by new problems, aesthetically sensitive, and dedicated to their tasks. But when viewing these characteristics in their unity, one discovers that they are not merely of intellectual and psychological, but also of ethical character. Somehow they all have to do not only with creativity, but also with maturity. I may here emphasize the following qualities.

There has been no truly productive person—even if we descend from the level of genius to that of ordinary talent—who is not at certain times totally involved in the work he wants to do. In consequence of this total involvement the rational and conscious part is fed by emotional, subconscious or subliminal qualities of the personality.

The result, then, is a tuning of the whole person to an acute sensitivity to all vibrations within and around him. Of course, certain hours of extreme concentration have to be

---

[3]See Donald W. MacKinnon, "What Makes a Person Creative?" *Saturday Review*, February 10, 1962, and J. P. Guilford, "Factors that Aid and Hinder Creativity," *Teachers College Record*, February 1962.

set apart for the final execution of the plan. The forces of creation work from all sides. This tuning explains why the creative person, once he has concentrated on his subject, meets enriching suggestions everywhere, in conversations, newspapers, in Nature and in books, as if the whole world shared his interest.

We may find here the explanation of a theological conception that has lost its meaning for many of us. This is the concept of "grace." Grace, of course, refers to the supernatural. It denotes the influence of the divine in the open vessel of the human soul, the unmerited kindness by which God answers man's yearning for the absolute, or the meeting between the mortal and the eternal. Translated into secular terms, this phenomenon is the state of being receptive to an embracing world of spirit within one's own limited existence. Under this aspect, even the non-believer may understand what grace is, and he may also understand the despair of the pious of earlier times when they felt "out of grace"; i.e., closed, hearing no response, lonely and separated from the grounds of life.

If sensitiveness, openness and involvement are the marks of the creative man, then exposure to dangerous situations is also one of his characteristics. This is not the place to show how much all creative cultures have been aware of this fact. For the Greeks, to allude only to one example, Eros and the *daimonion* that worked in men of genius, contained forces of chaos as well as forces of form. If we translate old mythological wisdom, to be found already among the Indians, into our modern sober language, we may describe the creative person as one whose task it is to force into co-operation apparently contradictory trends: the subliminal, passionate and highly impulsive on the one hand, and self-consciousness, discipline and form on the other. The desire for self-fulfilment may obstruct the patience and the willingness for self-sacrifice necessary for the completion of the work; and the vision of the perfect, yet ultimately unattainable, may produce a torturing feeling of insufficiency and despair.

We call this situation the condition of creative tension. It is the result of a precarious balance, more precarious probably in the artist than in the scientist, because the latter thinks and works within a more stable and objective framework, whereas the former must compensate for his greater subjectivity and freedom.

On the other hand, tension alone is not the sign of creativity. If it were, the modern world would be a hive of geniuses. With tension must go an inner personal rhythm that might be called the talent for repose. It leads one to interchange work and leisure, seriousness and levity, intenseness and relaxation, and wakefulness with the sweetness of sleep. Persons in whom this alternating current is blocked are likely to break down under the gift which the gods had meant to be a blessing.

Friedrich Schiller, a most amazing worker even in the grip of deadly sickness, said in his *Letters on Aesthetic Education*: "Man is truly and wholly man only when he plays." To be able to play and thus to lift himself above the strain and toils of daily effort, was, for Schiller, the condition of humaneness, of art, and of creativeness. Only stolid mediocrity can drudge on forever.

There is also a deep connection between play, creativeness and humour. Just as play, rightly understood, so also humour is a liberator. Tyrants have no humour. But as long as it is possible, nations enslaved by them try to restore their equilibrium through humorous anecdotes. If the humour ends, the enslavement is complete. Then there remains only one remedy, defeat of the tyrant from outside, or revolution from within.[4]

[4]See Gordon W. Allport, *Patterns and Growth in Personality* (New York: Holt, Rinehart and Winston, 1961).

Naturally, nations lose humour for the same reason that persons lose it. They have abandoned their faith in their creativeness, their mission and their future.

But it is characteristic of the genius that, even under the threat of despair, he feels beneath the gray ashes the inextinguishable rays of hope and faith. This faith, however, is more than self-confidence. Rather it has at the same time a metaphysical element. For personal faith, in order to withstand the attacks of disenchantment, must be nourished by a fundamental faith in the worthiness of life as such, or by the conviction that, despite the constant menace of chaos, the universe is a cosmos (which means "order"). Hence there is no genius who is not religious in one way or another, even if, like Nietzsche, he is an enemy of the religion into which he was born. Faith, so Professor John Seeley says, "is surely the tendril on which life winds to light; failing faith, life fails of its vitality."[5]

In this wedding of exposure and faith, or anxiety and trust, we have also the explanation of the polarity between modesty and pride that characterizes the creative person. Modesty comes from the vision of the ever better that causes the agony of inadequateness; pride comes from the sense that some Mind works in the creative person greater than just a weak and isolated human intelligence. He is, in the true sense of the word, "inspired," therefore he can inspire other persons. He knows that no single human being has invented the art of thinking and the laws of logic, and that no one could create truth and beauty unless the universe responded favourably to his endeavours.

An anecdote about the philosopher Hegel poses the question of whether it was arrogance or modesty that caused him to give the following answer to the flattering words of a lady. When she told him how proud he must feel about

[5]"The Future of Psychiatry," *University of Toronto Quarterly*, April 1961.

being the creator of a great philosophical system, he answered: "That which in my system has come from my own self only, is that part of it which should be forgotten." The story about Hegel could be woven into a long line of discourse that would reveal the awareness of humanity of an ultimate cosmic creation from which flows all human creativity. I hope to expand on this theme, as well as on the content of this entire address, in a later book that would deal with the creation myths of the ancient cultures up to modern man's excitement about the theory of evolution. (Who knows that a hundred years hence it will be considered a mixture of observation and myth?) The book would study the metaphysics of creativeness from Plato's *Phaedrus* and *Ion* to the Gnostics and Dionysius Areopagita and his conclusion that all being springs from the grounds of the divine beauty (*Ex divina pulchritudine esse omnium derivatur*). From Dionysius, the discussion would proceed to the mediaeval and modern mystics. On the philosophical level, the sequence of thought would lead from Spinoza to Hegel and Bergson. Freud and Jung, too, would have to be included.

Such a treatise would also show that each culture possessed mother images such as *Venus creatrix*, Saint Mary and Goethe's "Mothers," and that each culture connected with the idea of creativity had various levels of light; light being the symbol of clarity and consciousness. Thus we find the notions of the earth and the womb, which suggest darkness; of dream and promise, which suggest twilight; and of brightness, shape and contour, which suggest day.

HOW TO PROMOTE CREATIVITY?

The complexity of the creative process renders generalizations as to the requirements most favourable to its growth wellnigh impossible. What is good for one man is not good

for another. Some need quiet and retirement, others need
noise and crowds; the coffee houses in the European centres
of culture were more valuable for the generation of ideas
than many big libraries. Some men need happiness and
shelter, others strive in struggle, though, to speak in ex-
tremes, neither fat comfort nor slavery have pushed the
world forward. Dignity, courage and a glimmer of hope
must be preserved. Even tough plants may be killed in
perpetual winter.

Essentially, the question as to the promotion of creativity
leads us into conditions of human existence too deep to be
handled by educational manipulators. When the mediaeval
theologians realized the inadequateness of human logic in
face of the divine mystery, they coined the term "negative
theology." We may just as well speak of "negative education" and become as modest about our educational skills
and methods as some of the schoolmen about their erudition.

Instead of keeping other people busy with our own busy-
ness, we should try to help each person to listen to the
creative forces that are waiting in him. As Thomas
Aquinas said in his *Disputatio de Magistro*, the teacher
should consider himself a gardener rather than a creator.
By no means, of course, should this suggest inactivity. Without a gardener's care a garden turns to weeds.

An enormous amount of literature has been published
during the past two decades concering one aspect of productivity, creative intelligence. After the dangerously one-
sided emphasis on "adjustment," we now hear so much
about the need for intellectual "excellence" that it might be
time to assert that excellence is rare, and that a civilization
needs also a goodly amount of decent, modest, hard-
working, and morally substantial mediocrity. As Lincoln
said: "God must have loved the common man."

The discussion of the requisites conducive to the development of the best in every man, whether of high or
modest talent, would be beyond the scope of this essay.[6]
Let us examine here only some related problems.

First, since Aristotle, probably even before him, men
knew that the world comes to them through the medium
of their senses. *There* is, in other words, the basis of human
creativity. But to what degree does our one-sided technological and intellectual civilization respect this fact?
Modern man is a consumer who rarely makes what he
consumes. If he has the money to buy, dinner is served for
him. With rare exceptions, even the producer uses his senses
only to a small degree. Perhaps one can stand life in an
industrial plant only by shutting off a large part of one's
perceptive organs, especially one's hearing.

Our schools do very little to counteract this process. Also
here the mechanical and the intellectual prevail; this to a
degree that the sensuous and manipulative types, let us
call them the "craftsmen" in the best sense of the word,
are badly neglected. They have to resign and to adjust
themselves in order to become acceptable to our test-ridden
form of schooling. But the young "intellectuals" who go
nicely ahead do not profit either with regard to the totality
of their productiveness. For in order to have their mental
qualities fully developed, they too should learn how to
touch, to see, to hear, and to form something with their
hands.

One has but to observe modern men to find how dulled
so many of them have become to the sensuous stimulations
of their environment. Only the big and striking impressions
move them, while the beauty that is in the modest escapes
their attention. Only a few who enter a room for the first time

[6]See Robert Ulich, *Conditions of Civilized Living* (New York: Dutton
and Company, 1946).

are interested in its pictures. They are just for decoration—
spots on the wall. And few seem to know the difference
between a room that embraces and a room merely set apart
from other rooms by a partition, or the difference between
a square that gives you the feeling of view and protection
and a place where streets get lost in a triangle. The old
builders and planners who had not studied at our colleges
and universities—why did they know it?

Too many go through a museum like walking clichés,
or they walk through a wood and never observe the im-
mense variety in the shape of the mosses at their right and
their left. They leave such delights to the art expert or to
the botanist, but by doing so they are just so much poorer.

In contrast, the creative person, whatever he does, is
awake to the sensuous part of life. Apparently, there is a relation between his productivity and his perceptiveness.
Even the individual to whom we could not ascribe the
quality of creativeness in a particular sense becomes richer,
the more he is trained to see, to hear, and to listen.

Thus, returning to the initial theme, which dealt with the
relation between scientific and poetic creativity, it is not
too bold to say that if the hidden artistic talent is not
appealed to in a scientifically inclined person, he will not become as good a scientist as he could be, just as the pros-
pective artist will not arrive at the degree of excellence of
which he capable if the intellectual qualities have been
neglected in his education.

Since the Woods Hole Conference of 1959, made widely
known by J. S. Bruner's already mentioned book, *The
Process of Education*, educators stress rightly the import-
ance of "structure" in the intellectual schooling of the
student. But the word "structure" (from the Latin "struc-
tura") means originally something that is visible, and we
still call a bridge, or a dam, or a house a "structure."
Speakers with the talent of speaking without reading from

a manuscript generally anticipate their address as something "structured." They speak of an architectural vision, of something like a cathedral with a broad base, a middle part, a roof and a steeple. And when thinking of great philosophical systems I am always reminded of something similar.

Might it not be worthwhile to investigate to what extent the understanding of a logical "structure," considered so important for the educational process, depends among other things also on an aesthetic quality in the learner? If this is the case, we may well think of overhauling our whole educational system, especially on the top.

Secondly, in many of the recent experimental studies, valuable though they are, I miss the insistence on what I may call the value of "meaning." Why do so many adolescents glide into an uncreative state of rebellion and carry this attitude with them during their whole life, remaining, as we say, "perpetual adolescents"? The answer is that the strongest motivation which a person needs after a certain stage of development, namely the sense of meaning, has not been procured for them. Schooling, then, becomes a process during which teachers constantly answer questions which the pupils have not asked, while not answering the questions they would like to ask, until the whole procedure ends in a morass of cramming. This is exactly the situation which creative men, especially artists, remember with disdain. The most creative ones become the most difficult pupils.

It is not necessary that meaning always reaches into the metaphysical, though the adolescent needs that too. During all the changes in French politics and policy of education, the Lycées and Collèges have stuck to the philosophy course offered during the last year, because there has been the opportunity for deeper interpretation of the material learned so far, for questioning, analysis, criticism, synthesis, and a sense of continuity of human effort.

But the awareness of meaning can also be provided in the learning process itself.[7] A student should not be presented with mere results. Rather he should learn how creative minds have arrived at the knowledge he is supposed to imbibe, in other words, the knowledge should change from mass into energy. The knowledge, then, is no longer isolated but stands within a dynamic continuum. The same effect comes about—as a matter of fact, it is closely connected with the just-suggested historical approach—when a student understands the principles and the methods which have guided the seekers on their search toward wisdom. He thus envisages the single subject as part of a larger system of organization which, applied to similar constellations of facts and ideas, can be extended into ever widening areas of thought. The student then feels that he is in possession of a mental instrument he can use without foreign help. He is encouraged to become an explorer in his own right. He leaves the state of passivity for the state of activity—which is probably the simplest formula which one can find for education. He will then understand why the seventeenth and eighteenth centuries were times of unusual hope and excitement in science, art and politics, why every great philosopher of that period wrote a treatise or a chapter on "method," and why even highly intelligent men thought that just a little more education and rationality were needed to lead mankind out of magic and fear towards the path of progress. This was an error, but one of the grandest ever committed by man, and in spite of all disappointments certainly more productive than our modern tendency toward a new irrationality.

Many of us will remember from our own youth the delightful shock of certain intellectual experiences. The experi-

[7]Janet E. Forslund, "An Inquiry into the Nature of Creative Teaching," Boston University School of Education, *Journal of Education.* Selected Graduate Student Papers, ed. Gene D. Phillips, April 1961.

ence can even be outside any typical learning situation, even without any previously provided structure or system, merely the occurrence of a sudden jolt into the significant. I personally remember this sensation when at New Year's Eve of 1900 I was, as a ten-year-old boy, permitted to listen to a conversation of my parents with their friends about the gifts which the twentieth century would bestow upon mankind. Unfortunately, the gifts were different from the predictions. But this is not the point. For the first time I felt *history*. I envisioned generations before and generations ahead of me. I knew that a new century was coming, and my father told me that I would have to play a role in it, however modest, but honest.

A similar experience occurred to me when after five years of dull grammatical learning at a German Gymnasium a teacher brought a good reproduction of the Hermes of Praxiteles into the classroom. Apparently surprised at my interpretation, he entered with me into a longer conversation. Then I knew I had felt beauty and had had the chance for a dialogue with an educated man who happened to be one of my teachers, whom so far I had considered my natural enemies. The rebellious adolescent then became a serious, though highly capricious, student.

Many psychologists would explain such a change as motivated by a sense of satisfaction and pride. But pride in what? Pride at being accepted by one's elders? Probably, to a degree. But the cause was deeper. Every interpreter of the educative process will remain on the surface when he conceives of human motives mainly or only in utilitarian terms. There is more in humanity.

What we need is a holistic psychology, or to call it by a modern term, a "philosophical anthropology," which understands the creative process in man as the highest expression of an ultimately mysterious, yet all-pervading force. This force appears to aim beyond the amorphous towards the structured, beyond the unconscious towards the conscious, beyond the instinctive towards the self-regulating, and beyond the passive towards the creative. Would it be too bold to say: beyond bondage towards freedom?

All creativity is a form of liberation. For the creative man acts as a liberator when he lifts himself and mankind, of which he is a part, above that which is given towards that which can and should be done. But today the gift of intelligence has developed so one-sidedly that man can use it for total destruction of the delicate bridges between mind and Nature, between knowledge and the deeper self, in other words, between external civilization and the true *cultura animi*.

Here is the historical task of the modern school. It is to foster intelligence, articulation and specialization, but at the same time it must preserve the wholeness and the holiness of life. Naturally, when thinking of the higher stages of creativity, we think primarily of the institutions of advanced learning, although I would be unable to say what is more conducive, or, if badly handled, more disastrous to creativity: the elementary, the secondary, or the tertiary level of schooling. Perhaps the greatest harm can be done if the still soft clay of the human mind is modelled by clumsy hands. Our most urgent task is to find some form of educational policy, call it "mental hygiene" in the most serious and comprehensive sense of the word, which widens and deepens while it teaches to concentrate; which directs attention to the detail while it lets system and meaning shine through the isolated; which orchestrates while it divides; and which thinks of building a house while it assembles the bricks.

We should ask ourselves one question. Why could the Indians, the Chinese, the Greeks and the Jews, who in comparison to us knew so little, produce so much? Almost all we possess in spiritual wisdom and creative symbolism comes from them or is a paraphrase of their insights. Did they so totally exhaust the mines of the spirit that there are no more treasures to discover?

No doubt, the division of work will go on. The scientists, as one of them said, "cannot cut their brains out." Supported by anxious governments, they will constantly improve their methods of research. The artists will seek new forms of expression; and technology will produce new machines. Confronted by this, we must educate a generation that realizes the danger as well as the necessity of specialization and efficiency. Both will finally destroy us, spiritually and perhaps physically, unless human intelligence regains its capacity of weighing its creations and effects in relation to the creative order which we imagine to exist in the process of life and in the progress of humanity.

About the present situation in our colleges and universities we should have no illusions. We have in many fields a deplorable departmentalization and proliferation of inert research. The money which during the past decades has been given for totally useless experiments, the number of reports written but not read, the endless repetition of rapidly antiquated knowledge (instead of the rediscovery of ancient wisdom)—all this is frightening. So is the toleration of academic interests that force the students into courses that could well be replaced by the reading of good books. While the sciences have their more or less self-regulatory structure and sequence, the greatest confusion reigns in the so-called "liberal arts," equalled only by the study where the responsibility to the younger generation is most immediate, namely education.

For a hundred years American teachers have laboured devotedly for the unity and the progress of America, constantly improving the level of general enlightenment. But they could have done much better if they had not been driven from one so-called philosophy to another, from one teaching device to another, if they had not yielded rather helplessly to any kind of superficial criticism, and lived in departmental isolation. And this was often not their own fault but the result of the deplorable irresponsibility of many (generally not the creative) scholars in the liberal arts. Many of them apparently believe that a subject loses its dignity (and they their precarious social prestige) if it has some practical value and can be transferred into the learning of the lower grades. A problem of status is involved here, so illiberal and asocial, that it will require time to understand it in its whole nakedness.

Fortunately, the barriers have begun to break down. Maybe we owe it to the Sputnik and the fear of Russian competition. But the walls are still high enough to prevent the perception of many departments.

All this is not merely an academic matter; it concerns the creative potential of thousands of young people and of the nation as a whole. Confusion and unnecessary proliferation in the humanities, which are supposed to introduce the young into the treasures of the cultural heritage and to direct their teaching towards humane purposes, affect both our public and our private finances. How many families can still afford to give two or three children the education they deserve, without the parents undergoing considerable privations? Nor is it desirable that an increasing part of our whole academic youth turns into an army of stipendiaries. In the long run, democracy suffers from this situation. And with the crowding in our universities, and the subjects taught in them, we will shorten more and more the hours when the student can discover his own inner wealth by dwelling quietly on the depth of great works and ideas. The capacity of "dwelling on" was considered by the old Chinese sages the noble privilege of a human being. One of them, Chuang Tzu,[8] has left to us a parable that speaks so deeply

[8]See Robert Ulich, *Three Thousand Years of Educational Wisdom* (Harvard University Press, 1950).

of the temptations, of the mystical element in the act of creation, and of the identity of the creative mind with his subject that it may be quoted here as a summary of all that I have tried to say in this address:

A wood carver made a post on which to hang bells. When it was finished all people admired it as a miraculous work of art. Also the prince of Lou looked at it and asked the carver: "What is your secret?"
The carver answered: "I am a simple artisan and do not know of secrets. There is only one thing to be considered. When I was about to make the post, I was on my guard not to allow my energy to be diverted by any other idea. I fasted in order to put my mind in balance.
"When I had fasted for three days I no longer dared to think of reward and honour. After five days I no longer thought of praise and blame. After seven days I had forgotten my body and my limbs. At this time I did not even think of His Majesty's court. In this way I identified myself completely with my art, and all temptations of the outer world had vanished.
"After that, I went into the forest and looked at the natural shape and growth of the trees. When I happened to see the right one, the post for the bells stood ready before my eyes, and I could go to work. Otherwise I would have failed. And the people hold my work divine because my innermost nature became immersed in the nature of the material."

Lightning Source UK Ltd.
Milton Keynes UK
UKHW020022210722
406167UK00009B/776